Louis Lombard

Observations of a Traveler

Louis Lombard

Observations of a Traveler

ISBN/EAN: 9783337243265

Printed in Europe, USA, Canada, Australia, Japan

Cover: Foto ©Andreas Hilbeck / pixelio.de

More available books at **www.hansebooks.com**

OBSERVATIONS

OF A

TRAVELER.

BY

LOUIS LOMBARD.

AUTHOR OF "OBSERVATIONS OF A MUSICIAN," COMPOSER OF
"JULIET," A COMIC OPERA, AND DIRECTOR OF THE UTICA
CONSERVATORY OF MUSIC.

"When one goes forth a-voyaging,
He has a tale to tell."

UTICA, N. Y.
LOUIS LOMBARD, PUBLISHER.
1894.

Copyright, 1894, by LOUIS LOMBARD.

PRINTED AND BOUND BY
L. C. CHILDS & SON, UTICA, N. Y.

To
ROSE ELIZABETH CLEVELAND.
In proof of friendship and
admiration.

CONTENTS.

CHAPTER I.

SAVOIR-VIVRE.

Men rather than Things.—National Idiosyncrasies.—Other Days, Other Customs.—Travel, an Educator.—Snobs.—The Advantages of American Citizenship, ... 9

CHAPTER II.

LOITERINGS IN ENGLAND.

Sea-Sickness.— Liverpool.—Chester.—Shakespeare's Home.—Charlecoate.—Warwick Castle.—British Hospitality, . . . 21

CHAPTER III.

LONDON THROUGH FRANCO-AMERICAN EYES.

English Antipathy toward Americans.—Fogs.—Quart-de-Monde.—Vice, Puritanism, and Hypocrisy.—The Vastness of London.—Entertainments.—The Tower.—A Sunday Afternoon, ... 33

CONTENTS.

CHAPTER IV.
IMPRESSIONS OF HOLLAND.

Impoliteness of the People.—Their Love of Cleanliness.—Analogies between Dutch and German.—Ludicrous Head-Gear.—Tulipomania, 55

CHAPTER V.
DUELLING.

A Challenge.—Fencing.—The Absurdity of Duelling, ... 64

CHAPTER VI.
ACROSS THE LAND OF CARMEN.

Novel Scenes.—Bull-Fighting.—Living on Thirty-five Cents a Day.—Andalusian Girls.—Characteristics.—How to Travel in Spain, . 75

CHAPTER VII.
REMINISCENCES OF ITALY.

A Thrilling History.—The Error of France.—My Foolish Fears.—Venice.—Milan.—Genoa.—Interviewed Concerning the New Orleans Lynching.—Florence.—Rome.—Naples, 92

CHAPTER VIII.
PORT SAID AND JOPPA.

The Suez Canal.—Dirty Natives.—The Maroon Church.—The Danse du Ventre.—The Seaport of Palestine.—Horse-back ride to Jerusalem, ... 129

CONTENTS.

CHAPTER IX.
THE MODERN PALESTINE.

A Desolate Country.—Jerusalem.—Filthy Scenes.—Superstitions.—The Jews' Wailing-Place.—Urbanity Won by Subterfuge.—Over-Courteous Merchants.—Indigent Pilgrims.—Living in Convents.—An American Colony.—Beggars.—Mar Saba.—Sodom.—A Bath in the Dead Sea.—The Jordan.—The Future of the Holy Land, ... 140

CHAPTER X.
FROM CONSTANTINOPLE TO VIENNA.

The Golden Horn and the Bosphorus.—The Black Sea.—Stopping the Steamer to Dine.—Thirty-six Hours of Storm.—A Glimpse of Bulgaria.—Unusual Difficulties across the Danube.—Bucharest, ... 168

CHAPTER XI.
INCIDENTS EN VOYAGE.

The Influence of a Trunk.—Codfish Aristocracy.—Dishonest Courier and Store-keeper.—Hungarian Hate of Germans.—An Unfortunate Remark.—The Ignorance of Europeans regarding America.—Linguistic Blunders, . 184

CHAPTER XII.
HAPPINESS VERSUS TRAVEL.

Refining influences.—Diversity of Experiences.—Disappointment. 202

PREFACE.

In the hot haste of modern sight-seeing, these observations were inscribed upon hotel receipts, cuffs, backs of envelopes, and edges of newspapers, while the writing-desk was a camel's neck, the back of a seat in a diligence, or sometimes, Arab-fashion, my left hand. Therefore, it is hoped that the reader may not expect these jottings to be either exhaustive, or coherent.

Utica, N. Y., June 15, 1894.

CHAPTER I.

SAVOIR-VIVRE.

Humanity is so much more interesting than architecture and natural scenery that a narrator of travels might muse about men, at least, as much as about things. Of course, there is nothing new to be read in the human heart, whether it beat under the torrid zone or in the Esquimau hut. The same principles underlie all races, and selfishness, smoothened by more or less urbanity, "makes all the world kin."

Customs are good or bad only according to our view-point. Our opinion may be diametrically opposed to that of those to the other manner born, but opinions do not alter facts. Intrinsically, the practice remains the same whether we call it coarse or refined, for things are not what they are so much as what they seem.

While traveling, one cannot remove the epidermis of race, surroundings, education,—prolific breeder of prejudice. We cannot enthuse over the bull fight if we are Americans any more than we can enjoy dog-fights if we are Spaniards. The bitter English ale is nauseating to the Italian, and the glass of Munich beer filled with lumps of ice, as served in Spain, is far from inviting to the German. The Mohammedans keep the hat on and take off the shoes as a mark of respect ; we do the opposite. We write from left to right : they, from right to left. Mohammedan girls are often married in their tenth year; they are separated from all men but their husband through life. Even after their death, they do not mingle with the sterner sex ; one side is set apart in the family vault exclusively for the women. Some cannibals cannot show greater veneration for their ancestors than by eating their corpses, *sauce filliale*, as it were. The Dutch are the cleanest people in Europe, and yet I found them to be the most impolite. The Frenchman, reputed to be very courteous, does and says things that would shock the Japanese young woman who takes a piece of paper in lieu of a handkerchief, which she throws in the middle of the street after using. The American, who requires a cuspidor in every apartment of his house, thinks the Polish artist ill-bred, who eats with his knife. After this brief enumeration of national idiosyncracies, one may justly conclude that there is not much that is inherently good in the customs of any country if we except those social forms born purely from goodness of heart.

Etiquette varies not only in different countries, but also in the same country at different epochs; other days, other morals. The manners of gentlemen, however, differ only on the surface. *Herr*, *monsieur, signor, senhor, señor, khawageh,* or sir, means precisely the same thing : a gentleman.

Being contemporaneous with the elevated road and the pneumatic tube we cannot have the measured step of the scented and powdered wig-wearer of the eighteenth century. We dance the wild galop, not the dignified minuet. And yet, even with all their vaunted dignity and civility, our forefathers were not always above reproach, or it would not have been necessary to forbid expectorating into the pocket of a neighbor, or combing one's hair at church—which premonitions appear in an old French book on etiquette. But it may be well not to say too much about the peculiarities of others because "those who live in glass houses," etc.

Although traveling cannot eliminate all prejudice, it no doubt broadens the mind more than any other agency, provided one travel with the eyes open, and one be not too much influenced by guide-books and couriers: these monumental liars.

After seeing many countries I have concluded that the United States, notwithstanding their many shortcomings, are yet the most wonderful nation. History reminds Europeans that they were already rich with the spoils of countless conquests and the accumulated efforts of twenty generations at the time when, in chill penury, this baby government first saw the light of day. During the past century the dauntless American spirit made wealth, peace, and liberty, while obliterating King George's and Dixie's slavery. This country's achievements are the greatest of modern times. No one untainted by national prejudices can fail to see the advantageous substructure of American citizenship.

Yet, while traveling in Europe, I have

met many strange types of Americans--men and women imbued with the European disdain of things Yankee. They affect foreign tastes, manners, and expressions. Their mongrel accent distinguishes them. Their phraseology divulges its own unnaturalness. After having been abroad a short time they cease going to stores—shops, if you please. When traveling they only take luggage—no more baggage, nor satchel, nor hand-bag : only porte-manteaux, porte-monnaie. They would prefer to miss a good dinner than to ask a waiter for the bill of fare instead of *menu*. They pretend to love and appreciate all the arts. Heavenly beatitude invades their soul if a daub be shown them as a work of Rafaelle or Tiziano. The hallucinations of *fin-de-siècle* musicians are the only sounds their ears can bear. Such Americans are the laughing stock of their countrymen and a living source of scorn to the rest of mankind! The highest compliment you can pay to one of them is: "No one would take you for an American."

I pity the foreigner who draws erroneous conclusions unfavorable to this country and who rejects Americanisms with contempt. He has at least the love of his native land to atone for his stupidity. I loathe the American who copies foreign manners and echoes ideas and opinions tinged with European prejudices. He is a snob of the purest water and should be taught that simplicity and grace are the antitheses of vulgarity and affectation.

Among educated Americans there is no need of Europe's refining influences outside of the fine arts. No American can be ashamed of his national traits. Let him always lift his forehead high among the effete products of eastern civilization and fogyism and thereby enhance the prestige of his nationality in the minds of all men. The nearest approach to model citizenship has been made, in our century, on this side of the ocean, and he who can call himself a citizen of the United States can well afford to go about the world with his own characteristics and the pardonable pride of his nation's achievements.

CHAPTER II.

LOITERINGS IN ENGLAND.

I.

It may be that the cooking on board was excellent, but no one could prove this by me. Although the passage was a royal one, the sea as smooth as a mirror, I was more occupied doing politenesses to the fish than digesting. During the last voyage to England I ate only two meals and each consisted of corn bread and Apollinaris.

I know precisely eighty-nine infallible cures for sea-sickness, and I have tried them all. This may perhaps account for my being such a poor sailor. I have zigzaged every sea in Europe and some in Africa, and Asia, sailed repeatedly along the coast of the Atlantic, and crossed that ocean nine times, yet many kind persons try to console me with the theory that it is only a matter of crossing often enough in order to get rid of sea-sickness. "You will not be sick the next time," is heard on every side. But when I recollect how ill at ease I felt last summer on an inland canal, I brush aside this doctrine with ineffable contempt. I have been seasick even on land. From the time I secure my ticket for a sea-trip I am nauseated.

When entering the port of Liverpool one is reminded of that of Boston by contrast. In Boston the quays are only fit for landing fish, while in Liverpool they resemble a Roman aquarium on a magnificent scale. If the docks of Liverpool are the best in existence, the streets are not. They suggest those of the Hub; the same filth and tortuousness characterize the business thoroughfares of both cities.

I asked the porter of the North Western Hotel where I could hear some good music, and he recommended Music Hall.

I should have known better than to ask him. He no doubt spoke honestly when advising me to go to a place which would have answered his heart's demands. I must confess that it fell short of my own ideal concert hall. Music Hall! The name was alluring. But what is in a name? The lowest Bowery resort would put the Liverpool Music Hall to shame. A loathsome crowd filled the place, and the performance was in perfect tune with the grimy audience. I bid an eternal adieu to my sixpence, and immediately elbowed my way out into the scented air of the adjacent streets—into an atmosphere laden with the tangible aroma of rancid potatoes and stale beer.

The difference in the size of half crowns and two shilling pieces is hardly perceptible, though half crowns are worth sixpence more. I found this out after having cheated myself several times.

Little boys and girls harass pedestrians with: "Matches, sir! 'Alf penny, sir." They never let go until you buy. A waif followed me while saying in a tearful voice: " My father was 'urt on the railway—matches, sir ! My mother is sick at home—matches, sir ! I am 'ungry— matches, sir!" The haggard look on her pale and pinched face advocated her cause in expressions still more touching. Where could one better invest a "'alf penny ?" There is more misery in Liverpool than over-fed Americans can conceive.

II.

Chester is an interesting spot. Of it Hawthorne has said: " The finest old English village I have seen." And, indeed, it is beautiful and thoroughly characteristic, with its quaint, little old houses, the front of which are carved in multitudinous designs. Some of these queer structures date back to the ninth century. Many were once occupied by kings and queens.

Then they were called palaces ; to-day, shops, since they shelter prosaic beings, such as shoemakers, beer dealers, and the like.

The narrow streets of Chester, with rows of stores, above and below, present a unique aspect. You can walk through the principal parts of the town under a kind of arcade, not, however, as beautiful as that of the Rue de Rivoli but, in its way, fully as attractive.

With its imposing Norman Cathedral, its ancient towers, its crooked, mysterious, and low-roofed ins and outs, Chester presents a true picture of "Auld England." I must not forget the dilapidated "Mill on the Dee," which stands just outside of the city walls, near the castle now used as a garrison. I walked two miles around the city, the whole distance on the celebrated walls built by the Romans. From these one can see the most striking points of Chester.

The hireling, who piloted me for two shillings, pointed out Gladstone's country seat; the Duke of Westminster's palace, called Eaton Hall; the tower of St. George, whence, in 1605, King Charles saw his army defeated; the Providence House, thus named because during a fearful plague, the only family that survived lived in that house.

My worthy mentor also showed me the best brewery in Chester. There, at my expense, and with unequivocal gusto, he drank a glass of ale. From that moment he kept on pointing out other best breweries, but with no avail.

I am staying at the Grosvenor, not a large, but a charming hotel. Its spacious halls, with their tasteful tapestry, and the tidy arrangement of everything about the place, bespeak refinement. The service is good; the cooking abominable. The bread? Pugh! A mass of dough. I long for France, where one invariably eats good things.

III.

Stratford-on-Avon, the birth place of Shakespeare, is a lifeless town of 9,000 inhabitants. It is visited by two Americans to one Englishman. A beautiful fountain, the gift of Mr. George W. Childs, of Philadelphia, stands in the centre of the village as a symbol of America's admiration. Here after eight in the evening, every body goes to sleep except, of course, those troubled with insomnia.

The room in which the Prince of Dramatists was born is a narrow and dismal garret, fit for a Russian serf. In the house, however, kings and queens have come to do homage to Shakespeare. Glorious names fill the ponderous visitors' book. To do as every one does, I sat in the corner of the big chimney where Shakespeare was wont to sit. How could my meditations but be profound in such a spot! As to their being fruitful —the less said, the better. I am not susceptible to unconscious cerebration.

The school desk upon which the author of "Hamlet" learned to read and write is a big maltreated thing resembling an old ash box. From its hacked appearance one would infer that young Shakespeare busied himself with his pocket knife more than with his quill, were this table the only relic.

Being less poetical than Washington Irving, who once wrote that, having seen the place of Shakespeare's birth, he would not seek in vain that of his death, I visited the pretty garden in which stood the house wherein he spent the last nineteen years of his life.

The same mulberry tree that shaded the window of his library still extends its verdant arms. What draughts of divine inspiration were drunk under its foliage !

The beautiful Memorial Theatre stands within a stone's throw of the church in which Shakespeare is buried. Emblems of immortal spirit and mortal clay, placed side by side. A plain slab covers the ashes of the poet. It is said that his remains were not transferred to Westminster owing to the following epitaph which is engraved over his tomb :

> "Good frend, for Jesus's sake forbeare,
> To digg the dust encloased heare ;
> Bleste be ye man that spares these stones,
> And curst be he that moves my bones."

A bust placed against the wall by the side of the grave is regarded as an excellent likeness. The face is fuller than in all the other busts or pictures I have seen ; it is the physiognomy of the jovial companion rather than that of the book-worm.

The quaint figures under the benches in the chapel are worth seeing. The monks who carved them had as strange a notion of artistic design as those sculptors who were employed upon the Cathedral at Strasburg. I do not recommend these interesting images to those who place " trousers on the legs of the piano."

B

We all know that Shakespeare often drank one too many, and that he wantonly shot a deer in Charlecoate, but what of that? Many other geniuses have led a life not wholly blameless. In its uncontrollable gratitude for the scientific discoveries, the beautiful images, or the intellectual impetus it receives from geniuses, the world forgives and forgets the sins of these mental giants.

In ethics, politics, history, religion, philosophy, literature, art, in a word, in anything that is or that may be imagined, Shakespeare may be consulted. He is the universal book of reference. It is puerile to write his praises. In fact, to admire that which the concensus of opinion admires may be regarded as vanity. Xenophon said: "He is wise who knows what is wise," and some critics, knowing this, applaud every celebrated name without investigating the cause of its celebrity. They know it looks well to be in touch with the great : by praising them, they expect, at least, to show that they keep good company.

One, however, does not need to do this regarding Shakespeare. His genius is so overpowering that nothing but sincerity is brought forth. The critic enthuses because he cannot do otherwise.

Homer sang grand songs. Dante, with his sad, solemn, awful thoughts, moved men profoundly. Milton beheld visions never before seen. Cervantes, Goethe, Victor Hugo, all wrote with burning words. But greater than all combined was Shakespeare—the supreme interpreter of human nature !

IV.

On a perfect October afternoon, on one of those peaceful days when temperature, atmosphere, and sky are as in June, and the falling leaves seem to be the sole precursors of winter, I rode out of Stratford through the estate of Charlecoate. As I passed, many deer came near the road to gaze curiously at me with their large, limpid eyes ; while frightened hares, numerous as flies, hastily disappeared into their holes. I am on the way to Warwick, the county town of Warwickshire. The phaeton stops before an inn, and the driver asks if I care to rest an instant. This results to him in a glass of beer, as he expected.

Warwick Castle, with its imposing walls and priceless treasures, with its bloodcurdling legends which generation has whispered to generation by the fireside of every English home, Warwick Castle, with all its grandeur of size and its historical associations, does not appear so magnificent when one has just come from the humble house of Shakespeare. This grows larger and nobler in the imagination until it overshadows even the grandest feudal mansions of England.

The situation of the castle overhanging the Avon is picturesque. With its Cæsar's Tower, its Gateway Tower, and its Guy's Tower, each rising over one hundred feet, this historic abode of England's most famous earls, makes a sublime impression.

As early as the year 50, a fortress was built on this site by P. Octavius Scapula. It was torn down by the Danes, and in 915 Ethelfleda, daughter of Alfred, built the fortress on which stands the present castle.

Guy, the most famous of the earls of Warwick, is brought at once to one's recollection. Symbols of his powers and prowess still remain to startle the visitor, in the forms of a mammoth helmet, a furnace-like pot, and a monstrous fork, — objects which he used daily with ease, and which would have been large enough for Swift's king of Brobdingnag.

One morning I took the tramway to

Leamington, which is about two miles distant. It is a pretty watering-place, called the Royal Spa. At a music store I was informed that the best pianos obtainable in England were made in America, but that there was little demand for them, because the nobility itself could not afford to pay the price asked for such instruments. "Why," said the dealer, "here is an excellent German Grand, the best piano in our house; we sell this for eighty guineas, and the very 'gentry' require at least three years' time to pay for it."

v.

British hospitality! What sweet remembrances the mere word evokes! Without the perfect French courteousness, the obsequious Spanish politeness, or the good-natured American simplicity, your English friend takes you straight to his bosom, as if you were his own son.

For you, his house assumes its most joyous aspects, his wife smiles her brightest smiles, his daughters wear their prettiest gowns. For your entertainment, his women acquaintances play and sing, and his chums challenge you to a friendly tilt at billiards. Rare game is served, old bottles are uncorked, and the aromatic punch bowl scents the halls,—all this and much more, for you alone.

He was difficult to approach, this stern and rugged Englishman of sixty :
"With eyes severe, and beard of formal cut,"
but from the day I gained his confidence his great heart radiated the warmest rays of friendship. He did not inquire how much I was worth, except in character; nor did he ask what my talents were. Richer and wiser than I, he could gain nothing from my companionship; yet, at his table, my chair was distinguished by a silken *kuffiyeh*, and at all hours my every wish was anticipated. No more could have been done had I been a prince!

It is, indeed, well worth one's while to probe into the haughty and apparently cold heart: as snow-capped Vesuvius, it is aglow with fire beneath its calm.

CHAPTER III.

LONDON THROUGH FRANCO-AMERICAN EYES.

I.

Now, in London, in the greatest metropolis of the world,—greatest, of course, merely as to size and wealth, for as regards beauty, gaiety, art, and general culture, no Frenchman would compare it to Paris.

I am about to say some things that will displease English people, and particularly Anglomaniacs, but I shall give my honest opinion. Speakers and writers in England do not hesitate to express their views about the United States, however unfavorable these be. We should think ourselves fortunate if they do not distort or even invent facts solely for the fun of giving us a dig. Being an American citizen born in France, I may be prejudiced by the burning of Joan of Arc, the exile of Bonaparte, the war for American independence, and that of 1812. Remembering also the attitude of England during our war with the South, and more recently, during the Chilean imbroglio, my pen may dip unconsciously into gall. Should it do so I cannot help it. I have merely tried to record the impressions as they came to me.

The oftener I go to London, the more I like Paris. And am I unreasonable? It is now noon. A dense fog fills the streets, and coal smoke, black as tar, reaches into the inmost recesses of dwellings. This insidious soot defaces the buildings and augments the cost of artificial light. You must light the gas in the middle of the day. To cross the street you grope about as if blind. Your "cabby" walks alongside of his horse, carefully leading him by the bit. Think of a smoke-producing area covering more than one hundred square miles, within which, during the winter months, forty thousand tons of coal add daily to the thickness of a dark and deadly veil which hides the sun and then descends upon the city as a poisonous mass of hellish darkness. Can this atmosphere be wholesome to flesh or spirit ? It is a natural inference that it can do no good to the soul, though one may have no specific statistics upon this point. Too much smoke undoubtedly represses æsthetic tendencies, and oppresses the moral and mental nature of man. To prove its deleterious effect upon the body, it need only to be said that, one year, official reports gave asthma an increase of 220 per cent. and bronchitis 331 per cent. In one week the death rate, owing to the dense fogs, rose from 271 in the previous week to 353, diseases of the respiratory organs rising to 994! Dust of carbon is an easy vehicle both for noxious gases and organic impurities. The fogs of London, no doubt, induce consumption of the lungs of an incurable kind.

II.

In the evening, on some leading thoroughfares, an unending cavalcade of women of the *demi-monde*, nay, of the *quart-de-monde*, crowds the side-walks. Painted and withered faces, where the claws of lust, alcohol, hunger, and disease have left their ineffaceable scars, and from which has fled forever that sweetest charm of womanhood, modesty. Dolorous souls, more horrible than the pencil of Doré drew, or the pen of Dante described, flaunt their nauseous wares in the face of the world as hooks with putrid bait. If this be civilization what is barbarism? Of all the awful sights—and Marseilles, Naples, Jerusalem, Constantinople have some frightful ones—Regent street after sundown is the most awful. *Guarda e passa!*

Since all agree that this state of affairs exists and is a necessary evil, why not keep these women under police and medical control, as in France? To refuse to recognize the existence of a moral leper is no wiser than to wilfully ignore a physical one. Were it not better to confine her where she can do the least harm? If ignorance foster vice, what will not the avowed indifference of the state do? When virtuous mothers, wives, and sisters will realize the perils that surround their hearth, they will, perhaps, compel statesmen to stop their Tartuffe-like policy. Vice within proper bounds may become an efficient guardian of virtue; allowed to go rampant it contaminates its whole environment.

This false modesty, which covers its eyes and looks between its fingers, is the offspring of a narrow, hypocritical spirit, which, from the time of the Puritans, has fettered English-speaking races. Customs, religion, jurisprudence, politics, literature, art, all breathe its stifling atmosphere. But—I would better dismiss this theme, owing to the indelicacy of plain words in English. By the way, to observe the avidity with which English readers devour Zola's and similar works when in French, and to see those footnotes in French, in editions of English books in which obscenities are told, one would believe that the ability to read French is synonymous with low morals or that the mind of one who reads French is beyond further contamination. What think you?

III.

There are millions of charming persons in England, but, unfortunately, the traveler is not always made aware of their existence. I would like to speak of some conceited and overbearing Englishmen I have met, but I will simply quote from the London *Truth*. The following paragraph seems to hit their case pat : "We English are by no means a lovable race. We have many admirable qualities. We are a hardy, practical, persevering people; but these are not in themselves sympathetic properties. We are aggressive, self-assertive, purse-proud and hypocritical. We are apt to sing psalms and pick pockets at one and the same time, and our neighbors, not altogether unjustly, therefore, resent the over-righteous tone that we adopt in criticising them and their concerns. Wherever the Englishman goes he has the fatal influence of spoiling even the most simple of characters. A few British tourists will make the inhabitants of the most inexperienced province shrewd, suspicious, grasping and dishonest. This is within the common knowledge of any who have traveled in little visited lands, and a consideration of this phenomenon will enable us the better, perhaps, to understand why our neighbors, and more especially the French, so heartily detest us."

IV.

An idea of the vastness of the area of London may be had from the time it takes to get about town. I am at the Métropole, a large, comfortable, and beautiful hotel, though, of course, not so elegant as the Waldorf* in New York. The Métropole is not far from the centre of the city. One evening at 7.30 I wanted to go to the Crystal Palace. The cab started at once for a railway station, where I boarded a train. After a quick run I arrived on the grounds at 8:45, and fifteen minutes later I reached the palace. One hour and a half in transit through the city, and I had not lost one moment!

---

*As regards appointments, there is no hotel in Europe that approaches this sumptuous American hostelry, which might be more fitly named, a royal palace.

V.

I was not repaid for my trouble. Negro minstrels and a female acrobat occupied the stage until 9:30 ; then—eternal unfitness of things !—an organ recital began. Although the latter part of the entertainment was common-place enough, yet it atoned for the vulgarity of the minstrel show. During a recent visit I had the good fortune to attend one of the famous Haydn and Haendel Triennal Festivals at which, in the immense Music Hall of the palace, I heard the finest choral work the world can produce. Three thousand singers picked from the best choirs and choral societies for which England is renowned, and a magnificent orchestra with celebrated vocal soloists—all under the unerring bâton of Manns. Israel in Egypt and the Messiah were given as I shall never hear them again outside Great Britain, preëminently the home of the oratorio.

At Albert Hall I heard a very mixed programme. It was a concert by the Queen's Band of Scots Guards—an excellent organization—Mesdames Albani and Trebelli with Miss Trebelli and a pianist whose name, I am happy to say, I have forgotten. This combination might seem incongruous enough, but the most unfit, unsuited, inappropriate thing in this monstrous amphitheatre was the performance of Beethoven's "Moonlight" piano sonata. From the centre of the orchestra chairs, not far from the stage, I could only hear, once in a while, a loud chord. The rest I had to imagine. What those who were in the distant galleries heard, or, rather, did not hear, is not difficult to surmise. This musical instrument, the pianoforte, unless played in the proper place, and by a great artist, may be easily turned into an instrument of torture.

At Covent Garden, a very ugly opera

house, I saw the prettiest and most piquante Carmen, and the most ingenuous Marguerite conceivable. It was my friend, Zélie de Lussan, who for the past five years has maintained the reputation of being one the best prima donnas in England. And this is saying much, because, although the English cannot be called a musical people, they know how to attract the leading artists from everywhere. Indeed, London may truly be called the Mecca of musicians. While dining with Miss de Lussan I heard her say that, probably, she will never return to stay in America. Strange to record, she believes that good artists are underpaid there.

In London, where her home is, she lives in excellent style with her father and mother. Surrounded by friends and admirers, persons of influence and high social standing, petted and well paid by the whole public, what more can she desire? She is, in addition to all this, a prime favorite of the Queen, before whom she often sings privately. A short time ago Victoria sent her a photograph with her autograph. I do not wonder that this delightful songstress is universally admired. How could one see so beautiful a creature and hear so consummate an artist without admiring, yea, worshipping her.

Everybody spends an evening at the Alhambra, where a ballet is usually given. There, I saw "Algeria," a fine production with splendid stage settings and good music. Monsieur Jacobi, the conductor of the orchestra, had written the ballet music. He directed ably a body of fifty first-class players, nearly all foreigners, as most good musicians are in English-speaking countries.

At the Royal Theatre I saw Coquelin play "Un Parisien." This comedian's acting is so natural; his vocal inflections, facial expression, gesticulations, all simulate so well the result of inherent feeling that you forget the actor and sympathize with the man. Each auditor thinks he is the only person addressed. Coquelin has a private interview with me and for the while, under the spell of his magic power, the immense audience around me has ceased to exist. It is to me alone his tender words are spoken ; I shudder when he is angry, weep when he is sad, laugh when he is gay. He pulls so skillfully the strings of my emotions that, when the curtain falls, I realize he has made a jumping-jack of me. There could not be more science in his art, nor more art in his science.

VI.

The Prince of Wales was present and seemed to enjoy the play hugely. When a word, a phrase, a line impressed him he immediately translated it aloud to those in his box, evidently anxious to have his friends share his fun. After seeing his jovial face and hearing his unconstrained laughter, I concluded that this good-humored man would surely make a satisfactory king, especially with the fetters of the English Constitution about his throne. "Honesty is the best policy,"—when you are closely watched.

Joking aside. If there is any indication of character in physiognomy, the heir to the crown of England is the prototype of bonhomie. Many believe he would be preferable to his mother because he would make things lively in London, while she shuts herself up in her palace out of town. A leading merchant went so far as to say: "She is so miserly she reminds me of an old cook." Wonderful to relate! The Queen of England and Empress of India called thus by one of her subjects! So passes away earthly glory. Quite a number of Englishmen would prefer a republic, and some of them expect to see that form of government in England. Will the change be advantageous? I wonder, at times, whether our sovereign Irish politician is not worse than an English king. Surely the cost of regal pomp cannot amount to more than is wrenched from our taxpayers by unscrupulous officials.

VII.

What lofty thoughts the mere name of Westminster Abbey evokes! This edifice has been the coronation church of England's rulers from the reign of Harold, but it is especially important as the pantheon of the nation. The Abbey rises from the marshy ground bordering the Thames. Of much less bulk than St. Paul's, it is far greater in renown for its historical associations. The choir in which the sovereigns are crowned is a splendid specimen of early English; it contains tombs of kings. The north transept alone, however, shelters much more than all the rest, for there are the graves of England's most illustrious sons and truest nobility. There rest the ashes of dazzling literary lights from Chaucer to Tennyson : princes of the realm of intellect who need no storied urn or animated bust to make their last abode famous.

It was Sunday morning and I decided to hear a sermon in this memorable church. The preacher delivered an impressive exhortation to charity. He spoke graphically and with pathos, describing the misery of some little ones who were found the night before asleep upon the pavement, and nearly dead from cold, hunger, and disease. Poor children ! Forsaken under windows whence issued the joyful sounds of the dance ; cold in sight of blazing fire-places; hungry within the tantalizing fumes of a banquet. Can Divine Justice have decreed that some should have all and others nothing ? How consoling to believe that the rich were designed to be guardians for the improvident !

It is only when listening to sermons upon charity that I feel profoundly religious in a place of worship. Instead of wrangles and heresy trials, dear theologians ! talk to us oftener about moral philosophy disentangled from the meshes of your orthodoxy. Charity, 'tis the true Christianity. There is so much suffering ,in Christendom and elsewhere that, perhaps, your mission upon earth is to lighten the burdens of this world rather than to exaggerate the torments or the beatitude of the other. Do good, Buddhist-like, through personal abnegation. By your own living example inculcate gentleness in the brutal, and generosity in the miserly. He who practises virtue is nobler than he who preaches it. The lofty thoughts of Pascal are made loftier because they harmonize with his noble life. St. Augustine is great in character as well as intellect. Buddha, Socrates, Christ, Marcus Aurelius are beloved for what they lived no less than for what they said. Remember that your disputations will not prove even the very elemental principles of your creeds: the existence of God, the divinity of Christ, the immortality of the soul. Can, then, splitting dogmatic hairs bring thinking men to you? And will your abstractions impress the ignorant? Sectarianism has not done so much for the cause of true religion as softness of heart. Let human goodness prove the existence of Divine Goodness. And to do this, give not merely words, but give your life's blood. Charitable actions will win more men than all the rhetoric and logic from Moses to Leo XIII. He who gives to the poor lends to God.

VIII.

The imposing Tower of London was built in 1078 to protect the port and overawe the citizens. It covers about twenty-six acres. The buildings are mainly of the Norman period—that of

Henry III., but architecture of almost all styles which have flourished in England may be found within its walls. This edifice has been a fortress, a palace, a prison. To-day it is an arsenal and a safe for the crown jewels, the Regalia. This vast and gloomy mass of buildings recalls historical phases no less great and sombre. Here is the place where Anne Boleyn was executed ; there, the room in the Beauchamp Tower so celebrated for the rare carvings cut in its walls by those awaiting death. At various epochs these ornamentations were made with common knives by prisoners—pitiable wretches, often imprisoned for the sole offense of having incurred the antipathy of the king. And, if they were stupid enough to believe in the divine right of the sovereign, they must have found but little comfort in prayer, alas ! their only solace. In those dark days imprisonment in the Tower would have been regarded as a light punishment, had not the confinement there been the stepping-stone to the scaffold and cruel beheading.

IX.

The most dreary period in the existence of a Frenchman in this city is a Sunday afternoon. A cigar and the proverbial "brandy and soda" cannot prevent the sad, doleful, mournful, funereal day from invading his soul. With the son of Guzman Blanco, the ex-President of Venezuela, and a genial acquaintance from Havana, we were endeavoring to dispel dismal thoughts by relating our youthful escapades about the Latin Quarter. But this soon grew monotonous, and, with my Cuban friend, I started out for a stroll in the direction of Trafalgar Square. The night before there had been some rioting there, and, just as the most benevolent of men will tacitly wish for a conflagration, if there is to be a fire at all, so we, too, were hoping for, at least, a small revolution. Upon the square were crouched about twenty thousand ugly looking creatures. And what a motley and grimy crowd! Urchins, Socialists, Communists, Anarchists, Nihilists, unemployed workmen, and old women in rags, all listening to ungrammatical Mirabeaus. After a harangue the rabble would make a rush for the surrounding shops, being barely prevented from breaking into these fine establishments by a squadron of police. We were watching the guardians of the peace trying to encircle this *canaille* within the stone work around Nelson's statue. As my Havanese companion was remarking that it would be impossible in Paris for such a crowd to remain long undisturbed, we heard a howl suddenly arising from that human herd, as from a pack of hounds, and we saw the mob turn rapidly to that part of the square where we stood. Recalling the wise saying, "It is better to be called a poltroon after the war than to be a one-legged organ grinder," I at once suggested to my chum that discretion might be the better part of valor, and putting precept into example as fast as our legs could, we ran back to the hotel. Our silk hats having no claim upon the sympathy of the hungry horde, immediately became their targets. Stones, cabbage-stalks, and other missiles whose properties we did not stop to investigate, were hurled at us unmercifully. But the hotel was near, and we escaped unhurt, though unfit for appearance in any drawing-room. It was so close a call that we decided to remain in-doors for the rest of the day, satisfied with that much sight-seeing. The next morning I read that several workmen were clubbed, and scores of policemen stoned.

After all, thought I, a quiet Sunday afternoon is not without its charms, even in London.

CHAPTER IV.

IMPRESSIONS OF HOLLAND.

Were it not for the artificial mounds of sand, called dunes, which border the coast of the Noord Zee, the home of the tulip would have become long ago that of the sea-weed. The part of the country bordering on the coast lies below the level of the sea and, on account of this, the name of Netherlands, or low countries, has been given to the entire nation. Next to Belgium, I think that Holland is the most densely populated among civilized countries. Four millions of people live on an area of less than fourteen thousand square miles. If one have occasion to walk out in the country, he must always be very careful not to step upon a child or into some canal or pond. Holland is another Venice on a larger scale.

Industry, perseverance, frugality, and

a sedateness of manners bordering on incivility, characterize the Hollanders. I will record some indubitable proofs of their impoliteness.

The average Dutchman is taller than a Frenchman, and, being smaller than most men of my race, I created a commotion whenever I appeared among people who had not been taught to dissimulate their feelings. In the streets of Utrecht even well-dressed, and apparently gentle, women stopped in the middle of the sidewalk to await my approach in order to see me more closely as I passed by. Some went so far as to stoop, stare at me, scrutinize me carefully, and then exclaim : "Isn't he little !" This was a common occurence in every small town in Holland. The wonder of these good women might have been pardonable had it not expressed itself in so obtrusive a manner.

Perhaps it is the hypocritical education

of our day which teaches us to restrain the expansion of astonishment; still, this control of one's emotions is no doubt a mark of ascent in the social scale. Self-restraint, too, is an evidence of man's higher organization. Oysters and sponges contract as an effect of pain and dilate with joy to the point of opening. The Hollanders who glared at me reminded me of such low forms of life.

In London and Paris the most uncommon scenes attract little or no attention. The inhabitants of a great capital have seen so much that is odd or usual, ugly or beautiful, big or little ! A man could stand on his head on the Boulevard des Italiens without being noticed. A Parisian, while on the street, is especially unconcerned, except when a handsome woman passes. Then, can we blame him ? I am sure the handsome woman does not, if the Parisian belief that a women would rather be insulted than ignored, is founded on experience.

But let us return to our sheep to note one more proof of Dutch coarseness. This latter case, however, being an isolated one, should not lead to any conclusions unfavorable to this people. Yet, it was so unusual that I will mention it. A girl about seventeen years old, was walking towards me on a country road leading to a small North Holland town. When about ten feet from me she stopped, and, facing me, quietly fixed her garter, while I passed on, outwardly dignified and unmoved, though inwardly thunderstruck at so much innocence and want of decorum. It was indeed another fit occasion when to exclaim: "Evil to him who evil thinks!"

Perhaps the strongest national trait of these sea-faring people is their love of cleanliness, which they carry to the point of monomania. They dread dust as if it were the black vomit. From morning till night, and during the severest weather, you can always see people washing their houses inside and outside, and from cellar to roof.

Education here is well diffused. To-day, as in former times, this nation furnishes a goodly quota of artists and thinkers. Its philosophers, painters, and musicians have always played a prominent role in the development of thought and art.

II.

The knowledge of several languages facilitates the acquirement of additional ones. In some instances, when marked etymological and grammatical analogies exist, as between Dutch and German, the linguist learns a new tongue almost instantaneously. Vocabulary and syntax come as if by intuition.

Many years ago, long before giving any attention to the study of Spanish, I recollect carrying a lengthy and interesting conversation with a Spaniard, who could speak only Spanish. We understood each other thoroughly, although I was unacquainted with one Spanish word! My familiarity with other Romance tongues enabled me to express myself intelligibly, though incorrectly. In Roumania, I understood at once the signs on the stores, and nearly all the matter in the newspapers. The Roumanian seems to me a Latin patois. In the Netherlands, I had the same experience. The first time I heard: "*Welke is de Kortste weg naar ?*" and: "*Waan zijn wij nu ?*" I knew from the English and the German that these sentences meant: "Which is the shortest way to?" and: "Where are we now?" In Dutch the words *heden, morgen, gisteren* mean to-day, to-morrow, yesterday. Anyone, though only slightly acquainted with German, will hear the similarity.

To tribes of old Saxons, Anglo-Saxons, Franks, and Frisians may be traced the origin of the Dutch language. Flemish or Belgium Dutch, though closely allied to the Dutch of Holland, essentially differs in many important points. In roots and grammar it betrays more French influences.

I went about Holland without a guide, and found no difficulty to understand or be understood ; at least I thought so, and this belief answered my purpose. Objects to us are black or white if we think so. Perhaps they are red or blue instead, but if we were color-blind we would still think that we saw the right color. Misunderstanding is more frequent than non-understanding. We often fail to comprehend without perceiving our failure, and we complacently draw another signification. This is a common weakness with those who are studying foreign languages, not to speak of the millions of others who stumble over the same block in every walk of life.

In Holland, were one to meet educated men and women exclusively, it would only be necessary to speak French, for all such persons know that tongue. Many among them speak several other languages in addition. Hollanders, like Russians, are polyglots. It is natural that a nation whose language is not spoken beyond its frontiers, except by its citizens, should try to acquire the languages of others. It is a matter of necessity. Conversely, the French are the poorest linguists in Europe. They do not need to know another vernacular because their own is used in the polite circles of all civilized countries.

III.

The head-dress of the Dutch women is, perhaps, the most original in Europe. It consists of a piece of plated silver which covers the head, and over which rests a lace cape. Well-to-do wives frequently place a hat of the latest design over both metal and cape. That the combination is most ludicrous goes without saying. Talking about hats, I must relate a curious fact. A prominent London hatter recently remarked that man's head continues to grow until he is seventy, and that, consequently, he has to augment the size of his hats from time to time. This gradual growth is noticeable in all professions except in that of theology! Of course, I am now only repeating the opinion of the hatter. Those upon whose mental toes I may be treading through the record of this statement, will kindly apply elsewhere for redress ; I have neither manufactured nor sold head-gear, and therefore can neither prove nor refute this comical assertion.

Horticulture, strange anomaly, has always been a hobby with the Hollanders,—these innate navigators. Even to-day, Holland supplies her bulbs to the finest gardens in Europe. To conceive of Holland without tulips would be as difficult as to make an omelette without eggs. Tulipomania, a violent passion for the possession of rare varieties of the tulip, once seized the people of Holland. During the sixteenth century, speculation in flowers became as important as our own Wall Street transactions. One tulip bulb, called "Semper Augustus" brought the fabulous sum of 13,000 florins. A tulip bulb was frequently owned by shares. In a single Dutch town, it is recorded that ten million florins were gained in one year by the sale of tulips. The mania finally subsided, thanks to the energetic measures taken by the government to stop this reckless speculation, which was threatening to injure seriously the finances of the nation.

Haarlem is still the heart of the tulip culture, and thence numberless bulbs are shipped yearly to European and American markets. In the beginning of May, once, I chanced to be in the environs of that quaint old town. The air all about me was pregnant with the most delicious perfumes. The sight of vast fields of multicolored flowers filled my heart with gladness by the variety and gaiety of their coloring. The enchanting scene evoked some of the thrilling phases in the history of the tulips of Holland. Then I wondered how these tender petals could ever have been the cause of a complex social and financial problem!

CHAPTER V.

DUELLING.

I.

"The Christless code that must have life for a blow."

Just beyond the walls of Paris, one delightful June afternoon, I was riding in a street car. Absorbed in the contemplation of the varied and picturesque scenery which greets the eye of the wayfarer in the environs of that city, I did not notice a wagon in front of our conveyance. My attention was drawn to a cluster of dainty white cottages surrounded by their pretty kitchen gardens, when suddenly I was thrown from my seat. There ended my reverie. We had just struck a vehicle and injured the poor fellow who was driving. Numerous kind hands lifted the wounded man into a drug store and the car resumed its journey. A typical native seated near me, immediately began a seemingly endless tirade against the railroad company. "To add dividends," said he, all the while assuming dramatic attitudes, "what care they for human life? This is the modern Juggernaut. Where is our vaunted civilization? In order to save time the directors of the company become pitiless butchers. It is horrible, horrible!" He spoke so measuredly and his declamation was so correct that one might have thought he had memorized this speech for the occasion. And one would have surmised the truth, for the fellow was a lawyer on his way to argue the case of a man who had been injured on this same line, but a few days before.

Another occupant of the car, who happened to be one of the "pitiless butchers," to which allusion had just been made, since he was a director in this car company, felt it his imperative duty to resent the epithet, though applied collectively. He pulled out his card and politely handed it to the Parisian Cicero, saying: "Monsieur, you are trying to make a theatrical scene of this natural and unfortunate accident. Thus you hope to help the case you have on hand. Monsieur, you are a hog!" "And you, Monsieur," retorted the lawyer, "you are both a hog and a liar! My witnesses will call tomorrow at nine to arrange the details of our encounter." Thus ended the altercation. I did not learn the result of this duel but, from the records in similar cases, one may infer that no *accident* occurred.

II.

In all probability foils were selected as weapons. Every French gentleman is supposed to fence well. Apropos of this, it may be said that fencing has greatly humanized the duel, which, in former times, permitted every unfair advantage to be taken of the opponent. Of all the modes of duelling that with swords is the least odious, if conducted according to the urbane rules of fencing. It should not be thought that fencing is to be learned only by soldiers or would-be duellists; it is, above all, a social accomplishment. No gentleman on the continent of Europe would avow that he is inexpert with the foils.

The art of fencing is as old as mankind, but it began to be developed upon scientific principles only during the sixteenth century. At that time, the Italians were the best fencers; later, however, the French took the lead, by suppressing all the unnecessary and fatiguing movements of the Italian school, and by making fencing a mathematical science no less than a delightful art.

Fencing is, perhaps, the most satisfactory physical exercise; it acts on every muscle, and although the strain is greater than in boxing, the effects are more beneficial. It is the most healthful and the most graceful gymnastic exercise.

The expert fencer is distinguishable by the development of his chest, by the fineness and elasticity of his step, and by the ease and elegance of his carriage. It is difficult to understand why Americans have not taken up this pastime instead of boxing.

Fencing calls into play all the faculties, either mental or physical. In the twinkling of an eye you must measure your adversary's power; by his first movement you should decide whether he is a nervous fellow and whether his attack or his defense is his strongest point. You should also see if his guard is weak; in fact, your mind should be active quite as much as your body.

There is nothing rough in fencing, and although it calls for the expenditure of much energy there is no need of over-exertion. Persons of delicate constitutions can learn to fence well, while they gain strength in the exercise. To-day many women fence principally to develop the body, and to give it grace, strength, and elasticity. "Half of my pupils," recently remarked a well-known French professor, "are ordered here by their medical men—overworked students, barristers, and literary men whose livers got out of order, hypochondriacs and sentimentalists of all sorts. There is not a nervous disease which is not curable by the fencing master. And it is so enticing! Advance a little in fencing and you cannot leave it off. The first steps over, the task becomes a delight; the teacher has no longer any need to gild the pill."

III.

Though French duels are notorious for their harmlessness, it is pitiful that enlightened France should retain upon its social code so barbarous a survival of feudalism. In what does the modern duel differ from an affray between savages or loafers, if we except that mark of human puerility: good form? The duel is no longer an appeal to God; it is only to satisfy the supposed wounded honor of the combatants. Probed to the bottom, it might be found to be a childish sacrifice upon the altar of public opinion. Duelling was consistent in an age when men believed in the divine right of kings and priests. What can be proved by the result of a duel in our skeptical times? Nothing, except that, with tacit social sanction, a good fencer can kill the man he insults. Were we yet to believe in the intervention of the Almighty in the petty affairs of this infinitesimal speck: man, there might be some grounds for adhering to this mediæval custom. But Heaven is no longer called upon to proclaim a truth or to punish a lie.

A practice founded on the superstitious

spirit of a barbarous epoch should not be preserved by the civilized. Might is no longer right in jurisprudence. Blackstone thought the duel was "a high contempt of the justice of the nation, and a strong aggravation of the affray, though no mischief has actually ensued." Moralists and jurists will agree upon this point, though they disagree often as regards the morality of legal rights.

To the credit of Americans, let it be recorded that they abhor the duel, and regard it as a cruelty both absurd and meaningless, one that should be banished to innocuous desuetude, for to-day it has not the legal and religious sanction of the savage period which gave it birth.

The duel in France is the boldest symbol of human inconsistency. Frenchmen, they, endowed with so large a share of that most uncommon of all senses—common sense—still practise this unspeakable nonsense. Intellectual and educated men of excellent moral character, (barring out that particular immoral propensity to fight a duel), challenge one another upon the least provocation. And they do not fight for the mere pleasure of fighting, as some uncharitable foreigners might think. Frenchmen have not the instinct of pugilism so strongly developed as have their Anglo-Saxon brothers. Chivalrous, excitable, and susceptible feelings are the strong traits of the French race. These foster the duel in modern Gaul, and brush aside all the logic and culture of the nineteenth century.

It is a noteworthy fact that the greatest of all Frenchmen, Napoleon, was not a partisan of the duel. He was too reasonable. The King of Sweden once sent him a challenge, to which he replied: "I shall send you a fencing master as plenipotentiary."

CHAPTER VI.

ACROSS THE LAND OF CARMEN.

I.

One summer an uncontrollable desire to visit Spain seized me, and I went to Barcelona, Madrid, Escorial, Cordova, Malaga, Granada, Seville, Toledo, Burgos, and San Sebastian.

This visit was more than a pastime; it was a necessity—like the fulfilment of one of the purposes of life. The hope of sojourning in Spain had been for years a most cherished dream, and now I regret that this hope has been realized. There is no other land the anticipation of whose sight can give me so much pleasure.

Immediately after crossing the Pyrenees a complete metamorphosis takes place. When you step into Spain, you step out of Europe. The dress, the customs, the music, the opinions of the people, differ from anything you have seen or heard, unless you have lived in some Oriental country. The clapping of hands to call the servants, instead of ringing the bell ; the water venders with their earthen jugs ; the strange rhythms, weird melodies, and wild harmonies ; the dark, almond eyes, and long lashes ; the extreme courteousness in manners, and the abundance of florid metaphors in speech, all remind you of the Far East, notwithstanding its local color.

From Barcelona I took a train for Madrid, breaking the journey at Saragossa.

II.

One Sunday afternoon in Madrid I saw my first, and, I hope, last bullfight. It must be admitted that the sight from the start was very attractive. There can be no scene more picturesque than the entrance of the bull into the arena with gaily attired toreros, matadores, and picadores, ready with steel points, lances, and swords to infuriate the animal.

To see a bull and a man fight is interesting enough, but when the half-dead horses are brought blind-folded into the ring, for the sole purpose of being gored by the maddened bull, then I am ineffably disgusted. This sport is the most cruel relic of barbarism. I can hardly associate such brutality with the gentleness and apparent refinement of all classes of Spaniards. It has been said that the taste for bull-fighting was diminishing in Spain, and that civilization would soon wipe out this odious practice. As well think of Spain without sunshine as without bull-fights! Those inclined to believe in the ultimate disappearance of this sanguinary sport would soon change their mind should they ever be on a road leading to the bull ring on the day of the fight. The *dia de tores* becomes a holiday.

The city is all excitement. The streets on the way to the arena are crowded with men and women on foot or on horse-back and with conveyances of all kinds; from the most dilapidated grocery wagon, drawn by a phlegmatic donkey, to a royal equipage. Every available vehicle is put to use. To go to a bull-fight many *manolas*, they say, will mortgage their mattress, and I venture to add that some, perhaps, even hypothecate their soul for that purpose.

I do not like Madrid. It is too cosmopolitan. One goes to Spain to see Spanish things, but the capital of Castilla is a bad imitation of Paris where Spanish is spoken.

I visited the celebrated Escorial, a vast monument of granite built by Phillip II., and I could see no beauty in that gigantic and solemn edifice. Its sight fills one with awe and melancholy. There is not one line that relieves the eye as it wanders around the endless façades of this immense convent.

One afternoon I started for Toledo with the intention of going from there into Andalusia. Going over the bridge of Alcantara, with bright Toledo standing on the rock which rises hundreds of feet above the river, I was struck by the grandeur and uniqueness of that proud old city, which some historians call the oldest on earth. However, after walking over the uneven and greasy cobbles with which the town is paved, my enchantment soon disappeared.

III.

On my way to Cordova, after reaching a small station only a few miles beyond Toledo, my train stopped. I inquired the cause and was told that the express train for Cordova only passed on Tuesdays and Fridays. As this happened on a Monday afternoon I found myself with the delightful prospect of spending a night and a day in one of the most forlorn hamlets I had ever seen.

Although I had already enjoyed many novel experiences since coming to the country of the *puchero* (a mixture of beef, *garbanzos*, bacon, potatoes, cabbages, consumptive chickens, onions, garlic, oil, etc., which is served daily in Spain), I did not know that I would be obliged to subsist on thirty-five cents a day. This, however, I had to do. In my haste when leaving Madrid, I forgot to ascertain how much current money I had with me, and when I reached the only *posada* (inn) in the town, I found myself with exactly three and one-half *pesetas*—about seventy cents. This sum was all I could have until reaching Cordova, where bankers would honor my letters of credit. Having to count my pennies, I bargained cautiously for my bed-room. It was to cost twenty cents. For ten cents, in the evening, I ate some *puchero* and drank a large glass of Valdepeñas wine. In the morning four inches of *saucisson*, six fresh figs, and a bottle of wine again reduced my change by twenty cents. Thus, as I resumed my journey toward Cordova, I had twenty cents left for water, which must be purchased at the railway stations. And how glad one is to be able now and then to have a good wash when the thermometer is at one hundred in the shade and the dust blinding as in the Sahara! I would not advise a Sybarite to travel through Spain at any time, still less would I recommend a trip during the summer. It is so warm, and everything is so dusty!

IV.

But, here I was, and I decided to make the best of it. I was determined to see the Peninsula thoroughly, notwithstanding the dirt, the heat, and the beggars. In Cordova I visited the celebrated Mosque, with its many columns of rare marble. In Granada I saw the Alhambra, the finest Moorish building in existence. This is doubtless the noblest architectural conception. My next objective point was Malaga, because I wanted to drink some of the wine that bears the city's name. Thence I went to Seville—that is, to the heart of Andalusia, where I found the most gentlemanly men and the prettiest women.

The skies of Italy cannot compare their azure to the blue vault of Andalusia, and no other country possesses so many types of perfect human beauty. Almost every girl in Seville has the face of a Murillo Madonna, with the *tournure* of a Parisian *grisette*, for the Andalusian is as graceful in dress, manner, and carriage as she is beautiful. This lovely creature lacks, perhaps, the piquancy of the French girl and the versatility of the American, but she has, in a greater measure than either, ingenuousness, that ineffable charm of woman.

How bewitching the little Andalusian girls, with their snow-white skin, coal-black eyes, and pearl-like teeth, evenly ranged in a small mouth. And what little hands and feet! Like those of a doll. I remember one in particular:

"Un ange, une jeune Espagnole!
"Blanches mains, sein gonflé de soupirs innocents.
Un œil noir ou luisaient des regards de créole,
Et ce charme inconnu cette fraîche auréole
    Qui couronne un front de quinze ans!"

Could you have seen her beautiful head behind the strategic fan, you too, would have been fascinated. Did I say strategic? Yes, and with reason, for many a love battle is fought and won with a fan in Southern Spain.

V.

One more word about this great nation now fallen so low. Spain is one hundred years behind the rest of Europe. With her strange combination of fanatics and anarchists, this country cannot progress faster than her express trains, and they go at the rate of fifteen miles an hour, when they go at all! In Spain, conservatism retrogrades, while liberalism rushes blindly ahead. Here foolish and proud Don Quixotes, abject beggars, obsequious bigots, dishonest officials, greedy priests, fossil pedagogues, visionary statesmen, and illiterate and overtaxed Sancho Panzas, still sing harmoniously to the joyful twang of the guitar.

Yet, under all circumstances, and in all conditions, Spaniards are, if nothing else, happy. That which makes your stay among them especially pleasant, is their constant *alegria* (bubbling mirth). No one frowns in Southern Spain; everybody smiles. At all hours you can hear the tender and spasmodic guitar accompanying some semi-Oriental and gay melody wedded to words that tell how sweet life is *en España*. Had you heard such a song in the gardens of the Alcazar or of the Alhambra, you would have felt as sad as I did when I left these celestial haunts where each plant breathes a perfume, each sound is a song, each woman an angel.

All things considered, one cannot help loving these people, not alone for their contagious mirth, and their "devil-may-care" sort of existence, but because they are the most polite on earth: not so through mere forms of empty etiquette, but from the truest source of politeness—a generous heart !

VI.

If you intend to go to Spain, lay out your route in advance, and sail for Gibraltar from New York. While on railway trains sit with your back toward the engine, to avoid cold and cinders. Take as little luggage as possible. Our check system is not yet introduced, and your trunk may go anywhere except to its destination, if it be not carefully watched. Spaniards know that so well that they generally carry only boxes and large hand bags, which they take in the passenger compartment. These things often cover the floor to one's discomfort, for few persons enjoy sitting with their knees in their mouth. I was forced to remain in that position all the way from Madrid to Toledo.

At the station do not expect trustworthy information from employés concerning the arrival or departure of trains. Of all the men on earth the Spanish railway official is the last one who should be expected to read the future, for he rarely knows how to read at all. Have your baggage ready to be weighed, registered, and forwarded twenty-five minutes before the supposed time of the departure of trains. If you only make fifteen miles an hour on the fastest express, keep cool; your steam will not add to the locomotion.

Travel a little in third-class carriages, just to see how courteous even the peasants are, notwithstanding—strange anomaly! the filthy habits of many of them.

When selecting hotels, do not be influenced by guide-books. The name of the best may not be mentioned if its manager has not paid for such an advertisement. English or French is spoken at hotels of the first-class. The average charge is ten *pesetas* ($2) a day and fees to servants. Carry matches; I have never found any in my apartments. Expect to inhale the fumes of bad tobacco everywhere—even at your meals. Always drink the *vin du pays*. Do not hope for free hot rolls, butter, iced-water, tooth-picks, matches, lights, newspapers. You will perhaps be compensated for their absence by seltzer water, two kinds of excellent native wine, a great variety of luscious fruits, and good olive oil, which are served at all times and in every hotel without extra charge.

Take additional meals and drinks at the nearest *café*—never at your hotel.

For example, at the *café*, a glass of Chartreuse will cost four cents, if you do not divulge your nationality; at the hotel, where it is known, you will be charged ten cents, if you are French; fifteen, if English; twenty-five, if American. Generous fees to servants will insure better service than will fashionable clothes or arrogance. It is not so much, what you are, as what you give, that impresses the *criada* (chambermaid) with your importance. If dissatisfied with anything, express yourself in gentle terms. The Spaniard may be poor, but he is always proud. If you do not wish to be regarded as a boor, be more polite than in the United States. If you care less for cleanliness and comfort than for garlic and domesticated diminutive kangaroos, buy some insect powder and stay at *casas de huespedes* (boarding houses). But wherever you go, bargain in advance. In America, to be economical may seem sordid; in Spain, it is admirable.

VII.

Memorize a number of phrases sufficient to enable you to go about without the parasite called : European guide. You will spend less money, see a greater number of sights, and enjoy them better without this designing attendant. The knowledge of the French tongue will help you, since every educated Spaniard speaks French.

At the Custom House assume an air neither innocent nor guilty ; appear as you would before a photographer. Then open your baggage quickly and be patient; this may save you time and bad blood.

See one bull-fight, but do not express your disgust to a Spaniard. He is as fond of this sport as a true American is of base-ball. To retain or to increase his popularity the king or his representative must be seen occasionally at a bull-fight.

Whenever possible, ascertain the price of things before attempting to buy, and make your payments without a word ; the mere fact that you asked: "How much?", not infrequently suggests to the vender that he may ask as much more than the regular price as he think you will pay.

Carry a letter of credit. Find out the rate of exchange from another source than your banking house. Count your money carefully and test every silver piece. You need borrow no trouble concerning gold. The leading banker in Barcelona informed me that he had not seen a piece of that metal in five years.

Take a passport, but do not bother to get a letter of introduction to our diplomatic representatives, even if you can obtain one from the highest official sources in Washington. Such communications usually carry on their face the tacit hint: Do not mind this intruder.

In conclusion I would say: Learn in advance all you can about Spain and its people; buy a copy of the best guidebook ; do not start unless you have ample time and money, and in Rome do as Romans do.

I have not tried to establish rules of conduct for others ; I have simply jotted down hints as they came to me in the helter-skelter of travel. Like the ship-wrecked sailor who becomes a pilot, I am merely pointing out the rocks upon which I had the misfortune to strand.

CHAPTER VII.

REMINISCENCES OF ITALY.

"*En esta nacion, mas que se vive, se recuerda.*"

I.

The history of Italy forms a prominent chapter in the history of the world. It is the link from antiquity to us. One must look at this land from the retrospect. Each generation has left some sublime ruin which evokes vividly the thoughts and deeds of other days. Each stone becomes a tongue which tells eloquently some thrilling phase from the time of the Cæsars to the Middle Ages, or from the Renaissance to the Italian Unity. In these annals is traced more than the development of a race—it is the unfolding of humanity itself!

Before the seizure of Rome by Vittorio Emanuelle, and with the recollection of

Italy's former grandeur, it might have been fitting to exclaim: "How low are the mighty fallen!" But modern Italy, like the Phœnix, has arisen from her ashes. Freedom and education have dispelled clouds which seemed impenetrable. The sky is of azure now, and the sea is like the sky. Italy has been rejuvenated by her present government, which grants religious and civic liberties. To-day, her people live again in a period resembling, in many ways, that of Rome in her palmiest days. Certainly, the army and navy are a serious burden—like a ball to the country's foot. But then, they form a link in the chain of general peace, and the Triple Alliance needs them. They serve to preserve the equilibrium of European power; therefore, let the Italian army and navy be praised.

Guarding the temporal power of the pope was the criminal error of France. This, Italians cannot forget. Races in whose veins ebbs and flows the same effervescent Latin blood have been esstranged through the machinations of Napoleon, *le petit*. Much of the bitter feeling existing between France and Italy may be traced to this political blunder. A small commercial warfare is now waged while awaiting something worse. The French and Italians do not exchange their products willingly. Taking advantage of this unfriendliness between races which have every reason to fraternize, Germany sends commercial travelers from the top to the heel of the geographical boot.

II.

My childhood was passed in the south of France, where many Italian outlaws live, and, in addition to this, being the son of a Frenchman of the purest Chauvinism, all my early surroundings had instilled into my heart an intense distrust, if not hate, of the Italian character; so much so that I used to regard as accidents of fortune the gentle and honest

Italians I had known before visiting their country. I had a vague apprehension that all Italians were either brigands or organ grinders. This is as sad as ridiculous, but I am not the only one who, living along the Riviera, has been led to such uncharitable conjectures by a national prejudice which newspapers and politicians do so much to propagate. How could a child escape influences which reached all classes of adults? It is true that the vile Italian population which infests Marseilles—perhaps the most lawless in Europe—had helped to increase this mistrust. I knew, too, that in European statistics Italy held the first rank for murders. She has 9.53 convicts for 100,000 inhabitants, while Spain has only 8.25, Hungary 6.73, Austria 2.44, France 1.54, Belgium 1.44, Germany 1.12, and England 0.71.

With a dim recollection of some such

facts highly colored by my own imagination, I arrived in Italy for the first time. One very dark winter night I found myself walking alone in the tortuous and narrow streets of Vintimiglia in quest of a restaurant. My right hand in my overcoat pocket was nervously clutching a small revolver, but this means of defense did not reassure me. Each of the many tall and gloomy buildings was casting shadows which seemed to portend evil ; behind each pillar I fancied an assassin. The reverberation of the sound waves caused by my foot-steps appeared to me like the nimble tread at my heel of some black-mantled villain. Yet, I reached the inn unharmed, and there, instead of a den of thieves, I found a joyful and polite company in which I was well treated at a small cost.

Although I was quite young at the time I entertained these foolish fears, I cannot, to this day, refrain from feeling mortified at the remembrance of the injustice I had done these good people. But this youthful silliness was dispelled long ago. After frequent journeys from the Alps to the Vesuvius, and from the Adriatic to the Mediterranean, during which I met, almost invariably, with courteousness, gentleness, and even, generosity, my false impressions have been effaced. I have now learned to admire and love many Italians. There is so much of the noble Romans in them. The prominent nose, the piercing black eye, the proud carriage, the suave voice, the flowery speech, the elegant gesture, and the majestic sweep with which they fling the flowing cloak over the broad shoulder, recall their glorious ancestry.

It is unfortunate that there should be so many illiterate and lawless Italian emigrants throughout the world. They convey an erroneous idea of this great nation. There are more criminal Italians outside of, than in Italy. And the degraded type one encounters in America—the Italian railroad laborer—is never seen in an Italian city, not even in Naples. On the other hand, one rarely meets abroad the educated, intellectual native who, here, is ubiquitous, thanks to the thorough education his country affords. To-day Italian universities rank with the best in Europe. The highest culture flourishes again in its ancient home.

III.

I am yet under the spell of Venice's transcendant beauty. After having seen every city of note, I am inclined to call this the most interesting. It is, no doubt, the most characteristic. It is a prototype, a unique town. No anticipation can equal one's realization when reaching Venice. If a soul can be poetically inspired anywhere it must indeed be here.

Perched upon myriads of rocks, while her

feet perpetually bathe in the placid waters of the Adriatic, the original city of gondolas presents an incomparable aspect. Cozy niches will be preciously kept in the recesses of my memory for her marvellous churches, her incomparable Piazza San Marco, her sheets of blue water, and her light-hearted gondoliers. Can you imagine yourself in the centre of a busy town, and neither a mule nor a horse to be seen anywhere? The sound of a hoof, so familiar to us, would fall upon the ear of the Veneziane with the awful effect of subterranean rumbling, so novel and strange it would be. Silence here reigns supreme. The rhythmical fall and rise of the single oar, and the shout of warning the gondolier gives before turning a corner, are the only sounds, even at midday, one hears about the town. The gondola silently carries you through the city, along rows of weird but always beautiful palaces. Now you pass the Rialto, now the Bridge of Sighs. Under these far-famed structures, themes of many a song, your soul soars as high as that of a Byron.

No one should fail to see Venice; though he be pestered, as I was, by beggars and would-be guides. You cannot step without an offer of service or advice, however unnecessary both be. These fellows annoyed me much, but as I can say vigorous things in Italian, I often let loose the reins of my feelings and told these loafers, in a manner most unequivocal, to let me alone. Every time your gondola approaches a landing, one of these curs comes to help you. You protest against his assistance, but he is determined in either taking you by the hand and arm, or in steadying the boat. Of course he does all this if he thinks you are a foreigner; for no Italian would give one penny though he be even a prince. English people, and especially Americans, have developed this lazy class in the countries they visit. The fact that indiscriminate charity is a crime is exemplified especially in Italy. Many able-bodied adults of both sexes have found that it paid a better income to follow the carriage of an American with the request for *un soldo*, than to work. And they keep up the practice, to the annoyance of industrious Italians, and of wiser, though less chicken-hearted, travelers.

If the word "indescribable" may be fitly used, it is when speaking of the Piazza San Marco, one of the most glorious human achievements. No pen can tell the Byzantine magic and splendor of the Basilica, which stands on one side of the Piazza. The Ducal Palace, The Clock Tower, The Procuratie Vecchie e Nuove, The Campanile, and the celebrated Lion of San Marco are some of the many other dazzling, gorgeous, superb features of this treasure-heap.

Over the portal of San Marco, the resplendent Byzantine cathedral, stand four magnificent bronze horses, which, though lifeless, have traveled more than horses generally do. They were made in Rome, and Constantine took them thence to the city which bears his name. Marino Zeno brought them to Venice in 1205 ; Napoleon, to keep up the custom of conquerors, again took them and sent them to Paris in 1797. At last, in 1815, they were restored to Venice. While I was admiring these much-traveled animals, a lady asked: "Does any one know how old these horses are?" I at once seized the one great opportunity of my life, and exclaimed: "Allow me, madam, to look at their teeth."

IV.

In Milan I visited the cathedral, a forest of marble carvings,—artistic, grand. sublime! I also went to La Scala, the leading Opera House of Italy, and the true home of Italian opera. Odd to say, I only heard Wagner's "Lohengrin" there.

This opera was not given in the calm, romantic German spirit. Unless one can hear them in New York, Wagner's works must be heard in the country that gave them birth. However, the performance was highly satisfactory, notwithstanding its Italian color. As regards good singing, this execution of "Lohengrin," surpassed any I had ever heard from German singers. The orchestra, under Faccio, at that time the best conductor of Italian Opera, seemed, excepting some harshness in the brass section, perfection itself.

v.

Genoa is a commercial city, not an art centre. Yet it is not wholly devoid of art; it contains many imposing old palaces and these are filled with rare works. The Campo Santo (cemetery), which is about two kilometres from the city, is a museum of sculpture, rather than the mournful place so familiar to mortals. Art here seems to rob death of its terrors.

The Villa Pallavicini is one of the most interesting points near Genoa. After a drive of about two hours, with the sea on one side and hills covered with vines and olive trees on the other, you reach the villa, after passing numerous handsome palaces and country residences. With its many wonders and artificial grottoes, the Villa Pallavicini is doubtless the most noteworthy country seat in existence. It took eight years and four hundred and fifty workmen to complete this splendid establishment. The Prince of Pallavicini built it because his wife had reproached him for doing nothing by which posterity might trace their passage through life. Thus, one day, he said to her: "I have done something. Come to see." They saw, and from that time they staid at the villa.

I would recommend some of the dishes, in the Genoese style such as *ravioli*, and *tagliarini*. *Ravioli*, when well prepared, are the daintiest and most appetizing morsels imaginable. A dish of them sprinkled with good *Chianti* wine would make one feel the equal of a Rothschild.

Genoa is not the most beautiful city in Italy, though the wealthiest, but I prefer it to all others on account of the many pleasant acquaintances I made there. Not long ago I visited a friend who is organist at the Church of the Immaculate Conception. I cannot describe the power, nor the variety and beauty of the tone-colors, which can be produced upon the organ of this magnificent church.

*Alexandre Guilmant, who inaugurated this instrument, recently told me that it was the best in Southern Europe.

I spent a day at the sumptuous home

---
*See Observations of a Musician, p. 115.

of a Genoa banker. Having expressed a desire to hear the violinist Sivori, he was invited to dine with us. This celebrated virtuoso died a short time ago at the advanced age of seventy-nine. He was the last pupil of Paganini, and a worthy disciple was he of that master of masters! The youthful verve and feeling with which Sivori played astonished me. His tone was perhaps a little rough, but he literally spoke through his violin. There has not lived a greater interpreter of melody. His playing of a tender, pathetic air always brought tears to the eyes of his listeners ; his own were often moist after such performance, and he avowed to me that he felt intensely moved whenever he played music of that character. "Yes," said he, "I feel sad when playing such compositions. It is always a strain upon me. The grief I express with my violin impresses me as if it were real. I cannot help it."

When the artist himself is moved, then, and only then, does he make others feel the full power of his art. Certainly he should not allow his emotions to weaken or confuse his technique; he ought to keep a warm heart with a cool head. This Sivori did. In the performance of sonatas and concertos he combined with brilliancy and emotion: repose, dignity, majesty. With what pleasure I heard him play his own compositions!

There is a little anecdote concerning Sivori, which I do not think has ever appeared in print. I must begin by saying that Sivori's hand was extremely small, and he took especial delight and pride in the fact; not, however, as a woman might, not from an æsthetic point of view (although his hand was as beautiful as it was little), but because its smallness entitled him to greater credit in the performance of passages requiring long fingers. I met him once at three different epochs and each time he said to me: "You think your hand is small, do you not?" Then, placing his fingers between mine, he would show that his were half an inch shorter. The natural thing for me to say, which he always expected, was: "Maëstro, it is miraculous that you should play tenths and even wider skips with such facility. What would you not have done had your hand been of normal size!"

VI.

The editor of the leading newspaper in Genoa, the *Caffaro*, interviewed me on the New Orleans lynching,* which, though stale to us, was intensely interest-

---

* At the time of this interview the feeling against Americans was very bitter throughout Italy, and as I had expressed some opinions not too agreeable to Italian ears, it was with unmixed pleasure that I reached the frontier the next morning at about the hour when the *Caffaro's* first edition was being placed upon the threshold of the homes of *Genova la superba*.

ing to his readers, especially when treated from an outside point of view. He wanted the opinion of an American—a novel thing for his public, as all previous accounts of this riot had been blackened with Italian prejudice. Here follows a translation of the interview, beginning in a somewhat rhapsodical style, a manner quite foreign to our matter-of-fact journalists :

"A NORTH AMERICAN SPEAKS."

Do you know, O readers, Louis Lombard? Perhaps not, because you are not pupils of the Utica (New York) Conservatory of Music, of which he is director.

You indefatigable travelers might have met him sometimes in Genoa, or in Constantinople, London, Paris, Jerusalem, Cairo, Berlin, Monte Carlo ; because, though others may have the habit of remaining at one same place, he has that of moving all the time from one point of the earth to the other, except during the eight months of scholastic year at the Conservatory, which he conducts more through passion for art than for money.

Now, with the holidays hardly commencing, he leaves New York to return to our shores. Next week he will be in Barcelona, Madrid; who knows but he will end at the Canary Islands?

Until now, what is that to you; that a man should or should not travel, should leave or stay? But to me, who knew him for many years, the information that my North American was in town became a momentous fact. No sooner did I learn that he was in Genoa that I set all my reporters on his track to tell him I wished to interview him.

And my friend, when caught, submitted to the interview with admirable resignation and cold-bloodedness; one is not a Yankee for nothing!

"You do not expect me to relate to you in detail the New Orleans affair?"

said he, for he had guessed that it was my preferred theme, though an abhorred one.

"I do not expect that, because I know already too well how things went, and with what indifference the matter was regarded by many of you." Then, I added:

"At any rate, you Utican, though not Cato, you were too far from the scene to bear witness."

"We cannot regard this as a national matter, and my state is particularly free from any responsibility in this deplorable affair. In the state of New York there are no lynchings. We regard states in which they occur as very different from ours."

"Yes, these states are different, yet you are all united," I said.

"Lynching," continued Lombard, who noticed that I was not disposed to let him digress, "is not practised against any particular nationality; it is frequently resorted to to redress wrongs that a corrupt or cowardly tribunal will not punish." Then he stressed upon the fact that all the lynched Italians except two were naturalized.

"If there had been but one," I said, "that would have sufficed to offend us."

"Granting this, you should know that the Government of the United States could not have claimed quicker redress for its own citizens than that which Italy can receive." And here my friend Louis explained that the Italian immigrant can be naturalized five years after landing; that he renounces his own country, and swears to defend the American Constitution.

"It served them right," I came near saying, thinking of these renegades. Let me not proceed; they are dead and *requiescant* !

"Tell me, is it true that your state places especial obstacles in the way of Italian immigration ?"

"I am not aware that your country is singled out. Long before the lynching affair or any Mafia abuses, steps were taken to improve the existing conditions.

"In New York we have had for a long time an inspector of immigration, whose duty is to ascertain the moral, mental, physical, and pecuniary condition of immigrants, in order to prevent the helpless and criminal from landing, for such would surely become leeches upon our commonwealth.

"This system has been in force many years, but it is quite probable that it exists sometimes only as a dead letter."

Then I asked my friend: "Can you deny that since this New Orleans affair there has been a reaction against Italian immigration?"

"Yes, I can," answered he. "The severe restrictive measures which are being applied, are used just now against all nations indiscriminately. We are becoming more circumspect, whatever be the birthplace of the newcomer. And after all, I must avow to you that there are especial reasons against your people. In the United States, unfortunately, Italy is represented by its lowest classes; often by fanatics, felons, and others who would not be tolerated in their own country. While we have many intelligent and law-abiding Italians, these are greatly outnumbered by this rabble. I have no doubt that many Italians now in America would not dare to return home for fear of jail or of the guillotine."

Then I asked what regions were represented most. "The South, principally," answered the director. "And," he added, "you are represented by a most unsympathetic lot; by scavengers, peanut venders, hand-organ players, and the like."

"And our true artists, how are they received?"

"Very well, indeed. We cannot have too many of them."

"And our opera?"

"Ah!" exclaimed the musician, "the old Italian opera is at a discount now, if not wholly eliminated. Wagner and the modern French school predominate to-day."

"What are the favorite occupations of Italians?"

"Menial ones. Statistics might show a great number of miners. Then come those who work on railroads as laborers; never as engineers, conductors, agents, or clerks. The number of Italian farmers is very limited. Many steamship companies who incite emigration send laborers to help construct railroads. The price paid these men is lower than that which other nationalities demand. This renders Italians odious to many, especially to the Poles and the Hungarians—their leading competitors."

"Tell me something of your juries," I added, remarking that the main cause of the trouble in New Orleans was a jury suspected, justly or unjustly.

"Our juries," whispered he, "are composed of twelve men, who are occasionally selected from among citizens of questionable character, men quite susceptible, at times, to the influence of the mighty dollar. A jury is sometimes picked from a lazy class, because busy men find all kinds of excuses to escape jury duty."

Then we returned to the original theme.

"The Eastern States," said he, "hardly recollect a case of lynching. This means of justice, though barbarous, horrible, and illegal, finds advocates in the South and in the Far West, particularly in our newer states. In the North we think that legal punishment educates men to respect the law, while lynching leads them into contempt for law. We do not believe that a hundred citizens banded together, have any more moral right to kill than one single man could have, without legal process. It is strange that the old city of New Orleans should have given this sad example, and even more strange is the fact that those who took part were representative men. Your Italian diplomats insisted on an immediate reparation, which, they should have known, was impossible, owing to the autonomy of our states. In similar cases, even for injuries upon native citizens, nothing more could be obtained through our Federal Government than will be granted yours. In America, we believe that the jury was bribed or intimidated, and from the bottom of his heart every good American regrets the sad and tragic event."

VII.

I am now in Florence, *la gentile*.

"Where'er our charmed and wandering gaze we
    turn,
Art, history, and tradition wait to claim
Our deepest thought. Statues and marble groups
Adorn the streets; the very stones have tongues;
The holy fanes, the towers are eloquent."

What can I add in praise of this city? Were I the most gifted writer I could not do her justice. Such wealth and grace! At every step one is dazzled at her splendor. It seems to me that the masterpieces of all times are in the "Tribune," a hall in the museum of Dei Uffizzi, which has been justly named: "The richest room in all the world." In sculpture there are the Dancing Faun, the Apollino, the Wrestlers, and La Venus de Medicis. Neither antiquity nor our own age has equaled this work. She is the Venus of Venuses. It might be said of this statue that if it is not alive, it is the will of God; in form and facial expression no being made of flesh could denote life more vividly. In painting, one sees in this same "Tribune" some of the best works of Raffaelle, Van Dyck, Fra Bartolomeo, Correggio, Paolo Veronese, Michelangelo and Rubens. There are more marvelous creations in this single room than could be found in fifty museums.

In the galleries of Florence, Raffaelle's works exist in such numbers that were the well-known Dresden Madonna in a Florentine gallery no extraordinary attention would be attracted to this painting, which, in Dresden, being almost the only one of its kind, causes ecstatic admiration, especially among visitors who have not been in Florence. The theatrical effect sought by the arrangement of curtains in the room of the Dresden Museum, in which this Raffaelle Madonna is, may also artfully enhance the impression.

VIII.

The Count of Douville-Maillefeu, who is very well informed in European affairs, told me that the antagonism between the Government and the Roman Church was a mockery; that the Government was friendly, but that it would be impolitic to avow this regard for the Vatican. I can hardly reconcile this with the fact that the Mayor of Rome was discharged because he called to pay his respects to the pope, upon the occasion of the fiftieth anniversary of his ordination. This incident, by the way, gave rise to a witty repartee. Being informed that his wife had given birth to a boy, at about the hour when he received his notification of dismissal from the Government, the Mayor exclaimed: "*Je cesse d'être maire (mère) quand je deviens père !*"

Notwithstanding the serene aspect of relations which at moments seem to exist between pope and king, there still dwells the irrepressible spirit of domination in the heart of the vanquished pontiff. Within the walls of Rome a great volcano is hidden, not extinct. Its eruption, however, could not do lasting harm, thanks to the schools and the army which have thoroughly Italianized the few Romans who, twenty years ago, might have lent their sword to a papal *coup d'état.*

There is no more anti-Catholic, and I may add, anti-religious population, than that of Rome, and many say that the ruling church is the cause. It is possible here that the principle, "No man is great to his valet," may have something to do with the pope's want of prestige with his own people. Familiarity, perhaps, in this as in many other cases, breeds contempt. Proximity, and the sight of bishops and cardinals who frequent the thoroughfares and restaurants of the Eternal City, may tend to lessen the respect that these dignitaries would inspire, when viewed from a distance. The wisdom of the Arabian proverb, "Joke with a slave and he'll soon show his heels," is, I think, demonstrated here.

The answer given me by a driver will indicate the state of mind of many Romans, as regards things which formerly would have filled their bosom with religious awe. One afternoon I drove to the Santa Scalinata, a church which can be entered only by ascending one flight of stairs on one's knees. Determined to see everything, I underwent the pilgrimage. I must confess that I tried to facilitate my ascent by placing my foot upon the steps as I was lifting my knee. For this I was severely reprimanded by a priest, whose business is to watch the faithful mount in good form. "If you do not want to go up on your knees," said he angrily in Italian, "you will not be allowed to proceed further." Pretending not to understand, I pursued the "uneven" tenor of my way. Thereupon, the—what might I call him?—"step"-father gently took hold of my left foot and placed it upon the step, while, at the same time he shook his index vehemently from right to left in front of his red nose, which pantomime meant: "*That* is wrong." Pretending to be grateful for this, I begged his pardon with fitting gesticulations and continued the painful journey with exclusive knee action. I actually forgot what I saw to repay me for my trouble, so anxious was I to return to my seat in the cab. Happily, one is not obliged to leave the building in this manner; there is another stairway by which one is allowed the privilege to descend on foot. The driver was awaiting me at the door. Said I to him: "You may go in, too. I'll watch the horse." To this he answered, with extravagant vocal modulations so common to Italian plebs: "Thousand thanks! I'd rather go '*al'inferno*' on foot than mount to heaven in that way!"

IX.

"Where all, save the spirit of man, is divine."

I would echo willingly : "*Veder Napoli e morir!*", could I forget the coarseness, cruelty, and immorality of the lower classes in Naples. There, disgusting and enchanting scenes mingle at every step. Inhuman drivers, even more inhuman than the Cairo donkey boys; shameless females, depraved children, and dishonest merchants thrive in that southern metropolis in greater numbers than elsewhere in Europe. The thought that these beings should inhabit a bountiful land of almost celestial splendor, is hard to reconcile, even with the simplest conceptions of justice.

It is a common thing to see men enjoying the proverbial "sweet do nothing," while their wives, sisters, and daughters carry stones or drag carts. These women are well built and healthy looking. Many are very beautiful before thirty, but after that age some of them resemble Macbeth's witches.

Boys and men usually wear stockings and shoes; women never do. I have seen barefooted women, young and old, make mortar, break stones in the roadway, and carry heavily-loaded hods to the top of high buildings. In the place of horses, perhaps to spare these poor beasts, two girls of sixteen are often hitched to a wagon. In the meantime, the men smoke and play cards, if, as a diversion, they do not scold or beat the women.

Once I saw a sturdy and over-fed fellow rest his full weight upon the shoulder of his frail little wife while they were walking. The poor woman had a large bundle on her head, and was holding a child by the hand. The man was eating an orange. All this in a heavenly atmosphere and a luxuriant garden inundated with sunshine. What contrasts in one picture!

And yet I believe that our American girl is rarely so content as the humblest Neapolitan. A *canzonetta* is ever upon the lips of the Italian maiden. For this I thank heaven. The cheerful song takes a load off the heart of the stranger. It tells him that the abject condition is not burdensome because this poor girl, unfortunate though she is, enjoys yet the blessings of ignorance: she is happy because she knows of no better mode of life. Degradation and immorality have touched bottom under the fairest skies—in the land most favored by the gods. The plebeians of Naples are a living refutation to the fallacious assertion that the world is growing better. It is not necessary to have the pessimism of a Schopenhauer, in order to conclude that the modern vulgar inhabitants of that city have sunk to lower depths than the people of Herculaneum and Pompeii could have reached, even during the most corrupt days of the Roman Empire. Our contemporaneous type is more versed in hypocrisy, not morality.

Of course, I have attempted here to describe the *glebæ ascriptus*—those belonging to the soil. Among intelligent Neapolitans the conditions of life do not differ materially from our own.

From Rome to the Alps, higher types are found among the lower classes. As you approach Florence, you meet cleaner folk, and fewer beggars. And when you reach Genoa, you see clearly the distinction that exists between northern and southern Italians. From the Alps to Etna, the social strata vary more than the physical.

The depraved state of the lower classes of the South, may be due to the manner in which they were governed by their princes and kings before the Italian unity. The policy of these petty despots was to make these wretched people careless of the morrow, by keeping them in crass ignorance. And to complete the destruction of their moral and intellectual faculties, the blackest fanaticism was fostered, while the ugliest religious practices were introduced. Then, as ever before, wily ecclesiasts and despotic rulers united for the subjugation of stupid humanity.

CHAPTER VIII.

PORT SAID AND JOPPA.

I.

In Naples, I take a steamer bound for Egypt. It is six in the evening. A glorious sunshine still brightens the horizon as we sail into the incomparable bay. The sight I now behold will never be forgotten. Upon the placid Mediterranean, with the picturesque islands of Capri and Ischia on the right, and the multicolored buildings of Naples on the left, in full sight of Herculaneum and Pompeii, slumbering forever under the green and gentle slopes of treacherous Vesuvius, which, with his eternal crown of smoke, seems to boast of his infernal power—the most enchanting panorama unfolds, grows less, and finally disappears under a vast canopy of blue as Phœbus sinks the last quarter of his glowing disk into the Occident.

The next morning we were swiftly gliding through the narrow strait of Messina, leaving on our right Mount Etna, Sicily's renowned volcano, and two days after we landed at Port Saïd, Egypt.

At the Custom House, instead of a tedious examination, the officer simply asked me for *backsheesh*, (a gift) which I willingly gave to the amount of one piastre, (five cents,) and my baggage was allowed to be carried away without examination. Would it not be logical to believe that some Egyptian schools have given chairs to delinquent New York aldermen?

The affairs of this government are mismanaged, owing, say the English, to the opposition they encounter from the French and other Europeans, whenever they attempt to ameliorate the political situation. Can fair minded persons blame those who, prompted by the instinct of self-preservation, oppose England's rapacious policy by placing sticks in her wheels whenever they can?

II.

The city of Port Saïd, which owes its origin to the Suez Canal, lies at the extremity of a sandy and barren strip of land which separates a small lake from the Mediterranean. It stands at the mouth of De Lesseps' great canal, and derives its commerce chiefly from passengers on their way to India or Australia, and as a coaling station. Its population consists of twenty thousand souls, including six thousand Europeans. The architecture offers nothing new to one who has seen the hastily-put-together towns of Florida, but the natives supply all the novelty one's heart may long for. Dirty Arabs—dirtier even than Neapolitans—bask in the sun along the sandy streets. Men, women, and children crouched along the buildings among dogs, cats, goats, rags, coal, and wood, are heaped together in such a way as to puzzle the observing tourist who wishes to distinguish the organic from the inorganic. Little ones, with pretty faces that never were washed, sleep on the public squares—quite unconcerned and happy—their eyes filled with flies.

Nearly one-tenth of the Arabs suffer from diseases of the eyes, owing to their utter neglect of the simplest laws of hygiene. The lowest stages of poverty have been reached here, and the request for backsheesh is even more frequent than that for *un soldo* or *un sigaro* in Naples.

All the water in the houses has to be carried from fountains, where, at all times, men and women can be seen filling dirty goat skins. Since witnessing the operation, I have been thankful for being a disciple of Bacchus.

The entire face of the female Moslems is never seen. They wear a garb resembling that of a nun, with the addition of a piece of metal placed upon the nose, and a long black veil with which they hide their face at the approach of man, in obedience with a somewhat absurd order from their jealous husbands.

Nearly all of the natives have a smattering of French, Italian, and English, and those languages, mixed with their Arabic, form a most incomprehensible jargon, which they babble out with astonishing rapidity. They never utter more than three consecutive words in the same tongue, and rarely use the proper syntax. They will say: "No speak" for "I don't know," and "Good night" for "I am glad to see you."

Port Saïd supports one Maroon Church. This sect is Roman Catholic, and differs from the Latin only owing to the fact that celibacy is not imposed upon its priests—a privilege some wise pope conceded to the Syrian prelates many centuries ago, and thus retained them under the jurisdiction of Rome. Leo XIII. simply pursues the policy of his predecessors by his political intrigues. In all times popes have been diplomats.

I went to a *kahwa* (*café*) to see some Arabian girls dance. A small square room, furnished with several broken-down chairs of plaited palm twigs, four greasy tables, and a small bar, made up that favorite Oriental resort. In one corner, upon a ragged piece of straw matting, were crouched ballet and orchestra. After sipping a very small cup of imperfectly filtered Mocha, and paying my ten paras, (two cents) the strange performance began.

To the music of a nasal flageolet and a funnel-shaped drum, three young and well-formed women wiggled worm-like in endless contortions, while keeping time with the weird and monotonous melody, and adding to the orchestral coloring by clashing together small cymbals they held between thumb and index of each hand. Establishments that employ dancing girls are becoming rare in Lower Egypt, and in consequence, such places are usually crowded. Any one that has already found himself in a crowd of Arabs will readily conceive why I left at the end of the dance, vowing never to witness another. The stench that emanated from the unsavory assemblage was so atrocious that I felt an uncontrolable desire to be fumigated before returning to my apartments.

III.

On the 20th of January I sailed for Joppa, the oldest seaport known, and the great landing-place of all pilgrims bound for Jerusalem. From remotest antiquity its harbor has been the objective point of innumerable vessels, although its approach is exceedingly dangerous, and always dreaded by seafaring men. No good-sized ship dares to come within one mile of its port because of the narrowness of its single rocky entrance. Passengers and merchandise must be transferred to the quay in small boats, and it occasionally happens that pilgrims are unable to disembark, owing to a heavy sea dashing among the frowning rocks that completely encircle its bay; in such cases they are carried on to Beirût, two hundred miles beyond.

Fortunately, the sea was very calm, and I was enabled to land. Strong boatmen climbed upon our steamer and took every one, willing or unwilling, into their canoes. I, like the rest, found myself lifted off my feet by a sturdy Bedouin, who gently slid me down and rowed me to the shore.

Jaffa, of the French; Yappa, of the Syrian; or Joppa, of the Bible reader, proudly stands upon a rocky plateau that overhangs the dark blue waters, and, viewed from the sea, presents an enchanting picture with its many mosques and their pointed minarets, its snow white and dome-roofed Arabian dwellings, perched high against a background of the purest azure, dotted here and there with fig and palm trees.

Upon reaching Joppa's narrow, ill-paved, and filthy street lined with small booths, whence issue the foulest odors, one hardly requires the nostrils of a Sybarite to awaken from the dream into which his love for the picturesque has plunged him. "A heaven to the eye, and a hell to the nose," thus has the Orient been described by a writer, perhaps inelegant, but, nevertheless, exact. Disappointment is invariably felt upon close proximity to Oriental cities and villages, while at a distance they uniformly offer a beautiful view.

Joppa has passed through fearful struggles. Pompey, Alexander, Saladin, Napoleon, have each done her his share of harm. In 1799 the renowned French general ordered 4,000 of her citizens to be butchered and, horrible to relate, they had surrendered themselves trusting in his promise of mercy. Here, this same bloodthirsty soldier caused four hundred of his own sick men to be poisoned, rather than abandon them to the revengeful enemy. It is difficult to pronounce a just judgment upon this latter action of Bonaparte, notwithstanding its abominable aspect.

Joppa is interesting alike to Jew and Christian. From here Jonah fled to meet his well-known fate ; through here came the Lebanon cedars that served in the building of Solomon's fabulous temple ; in this locality lived, died, and lived again, Dorcas, the good woman, and Simon, the kind tanner, whose house is still shown.

IV.

On a bright Sunday afternoon I rode on horseback along a straight road lined with luxuriant orange and lemon groves, densely planted with trees bending down from the weight of their succulent fruits.

After having traveled about one hour among these beautiful gardens, fenced in with impenetrable hedges of prickly pears, I found myself in the valley of Sharon, facing the hills of Judea.

Along the stretch of thirty-six miles which lies between Joppa and Jerusalem, can be seen, at all seasons of the year, an almost unbroken chain of pilgrims—men and women of all ages, conditions, and nationalities, devoutly wending their way to their sacred destination. Jews, Christians, Mohammedans, all turn languishing eyes towards the eastern horizon, where lies the great city, holy alike to all—towards Jerusalem. Consecrated by Solomon, Christ, and Mohammed, it is the noblest and most ignoble landmark of man's divinity and iniquity.

Jerusalem, the cursed and the blessed, the sight of thy walls will ever awaken the deepest feelings; all hearts must beat faster and in unison as they approach thy gates!

CHAPTER IX.

THE MODERN PALESTINE.

I.

What other history can awaken more interest than that of the Holy City? Notwithstanding her present prostrate condition, Jerusalem still arrests the attention of thinking men. Here, at each moment, the breathing book of nature unfolds mysterious chapters, and now, as in the days of Solomon, a wondrous parchment unrolls itself before the historian. The capital of God's promised land remains a field of inexhaustible attractiveness to the religious and skeptical alike, with her strange annals and awe-inspiring legends.

Nine centuries before our era, began the decline of the Hebrew commonwealth. With the secession of the ten tribes, the decay of Palestine set in. From that time till now, Assyrians, Persians, Greeks, Romans, Turks, Crusaders, and others, have, each in their turn, stricken her without mercy. After three thousand years of bloody wars and bad government, the fair land of Canaan has become a naked, parched, and desolate vassal of the Sultan's Empire.

Instead of the proud, dauntless, and unalloyed race that once gathered around her bubbling fountains, we meet to-day filthy and cringing beggars—mongrel types of Syrian, Arabic, and European admixture.

The population of Jerusalem is preëminently cosmopolitan and her architecture truly kaleidoscopic; in fact, the only homogeneous feature about the Holy City is her revolting dirt. You no sooner enter Joppa's gate than the disgusting condition assails your every sense. The narrow and indescribably filthy streets are paved with uneven and greasy stones, over which moves an unsavory mass of human beings, camels, donkeys, goats, dogs, and hens. In the walls are black holes in which fierce-eyed merchants guard a few pennies worth of shop-worn merchandise, the whole suggestive of hyenas in their caverns rather than men in their sandal or spice stores.

II.

Now and then you pass a temple erected around something or other that silly tradition has rendered sacred. The finest building is the Mosque of Omar, erected upon the site of Solomon's Temple and around the Hanging Rock whence Mohammed ascended to heaven. The Koran records that the Prophet was taken away from Medina by an angel one night, while asleep beside his wife, and brought to the said rock, whence he ascended heavenwards. Twenty minutes after he was again lying by her side while relating his wonderful adventure. Owing to this legend Jerusalem became a second Mecca. Omar's Mosque contains some columns and ornaments from the famous Temple. Many Jews, Christians, and Mohammedans yearly undergo the hardships of a pilgrimage to Jerusalem, and with equal fervor these poor souls repair to their respective places of devotion; to spots rendered sacred by the childish imagination of the people or through the cunning inventions of monks.

A visit to the renowned landmarks of Judea has a tendency to efface the solemn impression made upon the mind by the reading of the Bible. Places that this book has described as grand, noble, and holy, become even to the faithful: small, ignoble, and unholy; to others, subjects of derision. The doubts as to the exact theatre of this or that scene, and the daily contention over its authenticity among the various sects here, evoke feelings of veneration in inverse ratio with the reflective powers of the pilgrim. From the time of Christ's death to the early part of the fourth century existed a chasm in the history of Jerusalem, which theologians complacently bridged over with the fancies of Eusebius and Jerome. About the year 325, St. Helena came hither and built a basilica over the exact grounds where stood Mount Calvary, the tomb of Christ, the whipping post, the stone upon which He was anointed, the cistern containing the cross, and so on. Everything at its precise place, and encircled within the walls of a cathedral of medium size. I should prefer to advance the opinion that the sacred relics and localities were selected to fit the architecture of the building, rather than allow such nonsense to pass unchallenged.

Proofs of human gullibility can be found at every step throughout the land of Israel. Footprints of Christ, Peter, and Mohammed are too common to be noticed, but marks of angels' fingers still attract the attention of some tourists. An appropriate pendant to Mohammed's rock is the plain near Jerusalem, over which, at Joshua's command, the sun ceased to move (?). One is bewildered and does not know whether to laugh or weep at such absurdities,—symbols that perpetuate superstition.

III.

The Jews still come to lament the loss of their paternal domain, where their nation reached the zenith of its glory. Every Friday, in a narrow alley called "The Jews' Wailing Place", they assemble to mourn over the decadence of their race. You cannot but be touched at the sight of these men and women weeping bitter tears while imploring the forgiveness of God. There is something sublime in the consistency of the Israelite character. Anathematized throughout the world during the past twenty centuries, God's chosen children still retain their hope in Him, and believe that His anger will be appeased, and that their former greatness will be restored to them. Such constant devotion finds no parallel in human history.

More than half of the present population of the city is Hebrew, and the principal trades are in their hands. Turks do not hesitate to take severe measures against the peaceful invasion of the Jews. The Mohammedan theory of fatalism is proving its validity every day, and it is the current opinion among men versed in Oriental affairs that Jerusalem will soon change hands. Perhaps the sons of Israel have an interest in the matter. *Qui vivra, verra!*

IV.

"Truth is occasionally recompensed and vice punished, exceptions which prove the rule."

I was visiting the Holy Land in company with two Englishmen, three American girls, and a family from Kansas City by the name of X. These persons, with the exception of Mrs. X., seemed friendly to me; they were, at least, invariably polite. But the Missouri lady did not seem to notice me. It was not exactly scorn that she felt, but I could plainly see that it was disdain. So much so that my two English friends, Messrs. B. and P., became aware of this. It was annoying, especially as I knew I was to be in in this woman's society for the coming fortnight. Thereupon I resolved on an expedient to win common urbanity from her, and my subterfuge succeeded.

One afternoon in Jericho three men met bent upon evil doing. They were Mr. B., Mr. P., and I. The conspiracy was to let Mrs. X. infer that I was a great author commissioned by the largest publishing house in America to write a book of travels. This was to be done by dropping an occasional word about this hypothetical book within the lady's hearing, while, of course, assuming the air of candor wags alone can assume. On that evening, at dinner, her bow to me was especially formal, yea, freezing. It was the proverbial straw, and Mr. P. was encouraged to begin at once by saying to me: "Why don't you print it in London?" I replied: "Because, my dear Mr. P., it is to my interest to have it published by those who pay me the most." By this time Mrs. X. was thoroughly interested, for it should not be imagined that her disdain had removed her curiosity; that were not human—femininely human, I would say.

The next morning we were riding rapidly towards Jerusalem. Mrs. X. was about twenty feet ahead of us. "I'll give you two thousand pounds for your book," ejaculated Mr. P. "That is more, I am sure, than any New York house can afford to offer you," added Mr. B. Suddenly the speed of Mrs. X.'s horse was reduced. To any one not familiar with the circumstances, this change of gait would have been meaningless; but it almost caused Mr. B. to fall off his horse, so funny did the whole situation appear to him. After regaining our composure, I said with all the dignity I could muster: " Gentlemen, I beg of you not to speak to me again upon this subject. I have a contract, and I am satisfied with the New York arrangements. Were you to offer me ten times two thousand pounds it would not alter my decision. I am legally and morally bound."

From that moment we did not speak again about the book. It was no longer necessary. The result had been attained. Kansas City was won.

The next scene in this thrilling play was in the morning at the reading room of the hotel at Jerusalem. I got up earlier than usual in order to prepare the stage settings. That no doubt should remain as to my being an author, I began surrounding myself with the paraphernalia of a busy writer. I took the biggest table in the room, clipped at random numerous pieces from old newspapers, and with my guide-books and those of my friends thrown clumsily in a heap, I improvised a work table adequate for Herbert Spencer and Shakspeare combined—so far, at least, as appearances could go. Four pencils, a pair of scissors, and a bottle of mucilage completed the apotheosis. Thus armed I laid low for my unsophisticated victim. I had barely seated myself at the table than I heard a pleasant voice say: "Good morning, Mr. Lombard." Whether or no it was a coincidence, the fact is that Mrs. X., too, had risen earlier than usual; evidently, however, with different intentions from mine. "Good morning, madam," said I as politely as I could, though I did not lift my pencil from the pad. Perhaps she feared to interrupt the flow of my precious thoughts, or perhaps she did not know how to "break the ice,"—in fine, she remained as mute as two oysters for two mortal minutes. Then she appeased her anguish and my own by saying in the meekest manner: "I know you now; you cannot hide your identity any longer. Of course you must pardon me if I have not been more communicative during these trips together. I believe that so intelligent a man as you will not blame a woman for being particular about her associates. How do we know who the people are that we meet with a party of this kind? Now, however, it is a different thing. I know who you are, and I also know that you are writing an interesting book of travels. What is the title going to be?"

"I am sorry, madam," I answered,

"but secrecy in the matter has been enjoined upon me. The title cannot be announced before the work is published."
"Yes," added Mrs. X., "but how will I know when the book appears if I don't know its name? I wish to know because I want to buy at least a dozen copies to circulate among my friends. You see, it will be so much easier to do this than to take notes while traveling. Besides I could not describe as you can. We are traveling over the same ground and your book will suit exactly my own purpose. But now, (here Mrs. X. became especially persuasive) my dear Mr. Lombard, promise me that you will not say anything mean about me or my family, won't you? You authors often write things so different from what you say in conversation!" With a majestic wave of the hand I assured her that nothing but praise could be written of so charming a woman, but I did not tell her the

title of the book. I simply said that I would inform her when it appeared.

From that moment until I left Cook's party in Cairo, Mrs. X. was very courteous to me, even obsequiously so. I do not know how she would act to-day should we meet; she must be so tired awaiting that book.

Many persons treat writers in this polite manner only when fearing to be unfavorably criticised. They act upon the wise advice given by a father to his son about to enter public life : "My son, be kind to the newspaper man."

v.

How can a man be more suave than a Jerusalem merchant ? As you pass near his shop he invariably greets you with "*Naracsaid, Khawageh,*" or "Good morning, sir," as your appearance may suggest, and, at the same time, he offers his hand, as if he had long known you.

When such a fellow first approached me I immediately fell into his trap, shook hands, and said a few pleasant things, all the while under the delusion that I had met him before. He at once began setting forth the superiority of his wares in glowing metaphors, and in a way worthy of a better store, but I soon stopped the flow of his panegyrics with the remark that I had left all my money in another pair of trousers, and made my escape. From that moment I resolved to abstain from courteous exchange of civilities with any shopkeeper. I learned that it was their custom to address all lookers-on in the same when-did-you-get-back manner.

Most of the impecunious pilgrims who constantly flock here are from Russia. During thirty or forty years they deprive themselves of the bare necessaries of life for the sole purpose of kneeling once at the shrine of Christ. The remembrance of the deprivations they have undergone is often obliterated by the sufferings they must endure before reaching Mount Calvary. Packed like cattle in small and ill-ventilated vessels, they sail from some port on the Black Sea, and after weeks of torture are landed at Joppa. From the moment they arrive they start on foot toward the goal of their devout wishes.

A Russian colony of some importance is clustered about Joppa's Gate, just beyond the walls of Jerusalem. These settlers improve the country by working the land and building substantial houses. They organize powerful societies and make extensive purchases of real estate.

The Russians have evidently come to stay, and their encroachments upon Turkish territory are viewed with unmixed favor at St. Petersburg. The Bear would like to secure a firm footing upon the shores of the Mediterranean, and his spies are lurking throughout the Levant with that exclusive object in view. If the other European powers ever become incapable of preventing it, we may expect a Russian *coup de main* over Syria and Palestine.

Since the last decade the majority of tourists has been composed of Americans. Among the European visitors, the English outnumber all others. Travelers of the best class usually go under the supervision of excursion managers. For a sum payable at an agency, may be secured a ticket entitling the holder to all the requirements of those who wish to "do" the Holy Land, namely: a competent dragoman to conduct him to the noteworthy spots, and, when necessary, Kawwasses and Bedouins to protect him. Hotel accommodations not being available everywhere, camping equipments and provisions will be carried by the servants. These advantages should not be overlooked by those contemplating a trip to the Dead Sea, the River Jordan, or Mount Sinaï.

In civilized lands, convicts are better quartered and fed than are guests in the average Oriental *khan* (hotel). After spending one week in the best hotel in Jerusalem, the members of our caravan found the agency's cheerful tents, neat bedding, and wholesome food as novel as delightful.

VI.

I dined one day with some French and Spanish prelates at the Mother Convent of the Franciscan Order. The table was excellent and the home-made wine very acceptable. Had I not been with Cook's party I would have taken room and board with the jovial monks. Catholics who go to Palestine always stay at Franciscan convents, when visiting Joppa, Ramleh, Ain Karim, Bethlehem, Acre, Nazareth, or Jerusalem. On Mount Carmel pilgrims are welcomed by barefooted Carmelites.

Visitors always meet with a hearty reception, whatever be their creed. The monks are pleasant and educated men. Contrary to the statement of some malevolent tourists, they never impose their devotions upon their guests.

It is the custom for visitors, when leaving, to give a small sum of money to the Fathers ; about five francs per day is regarded as adequate. Were I to return I should most certainly take lodgings in convents.

An interesting American Society exists here. Some years ago a band of pilgrims left Chicago, to come here and await the return of Christ. From certain propositions, comprehensible only to those "walking in the true light," they had deduced the precise hour of his reappearance. Through some error in the calculations, Christ did not appear. The sun ascended from behind the Mount of Olives and passed over the Tower of David without shedding its rays upon the Divine Man. At the time they could not ascertain the cause of their terrible disappointment. But Chicago people were not to be disconcerted. Another careful perusal of the Bible was at once undertaken and their efforts were soon rewarded with the astounding discovery that their calculations had been false. After weeks of untiring research, they unearthed the correct date. How? He alone knows! Meanwhile, money due them at Chicago was withheld by their mean and skeptical relatives, who, supported by the opinion of the American Consul, successfully argued mania, fantasia, derangement, calenture of the brain, etc., etc.

As the confraternity's time is occupied solely with praying and basking in the sunshine, its members naturally receive a compensation commensurate with their arduous toil. The sad fact must be mentioned that about fifty per cent. of the faithful sheep have deserted the flock since the alarming news came that Chicago friends could legally clutch their personal funds.

I met the thirteen remaining members at their neat and comfortable quarters and found them all urbane, intelligent, and well-informed ; well balanced on every thing but their queer hobby.

VII.

Every Arab is a beggar. The word *backsheesh* incessantly rings in the the visitor's ear during his sojourn in Jerusalem. No sooner can a child utter one syllable than it is trained to ask for *backsheesh*. Mere weaklings, yet in their mother's arm, will often be heard unconsciously muttering "*b'sheea! b'sheea!*" The natives regard the alms they receive from travelers as their just due. They do not beg, but simply collect gate money. A very small gift will satisfy the most beggars; indeed, the donation of one Turkish piastre will raise the giver to the status of a Crœsus in the estimation of the receiver. The reckless generosity of the man who gives two piastres is usually regarded as a sign of insanity. The existence of this hypothesis in the minds of Arabs was made evident to me. I gave several copper coins to an old woman. She looked at me amazed, shaking her head, as if thinking: "I am sorry! He is so young, too." And she went away without thanking me, so absorbed was she with the thought of my misfortune.

VIII.

The greater part of the area of Palestine is sterile. Sandy wastes and craggy hills meet the sight in all directions, and but for the narrow strips of cultivated land, which, at broad intervals, intersect the lifeless topography of the country, one might conclude that the pursuit of agriculture has been wholly abandoned by the inhabitants. Nearly all the way between Jerusalem and the Dead Sea the earth appears to have emerged from a terrible conflagration. The desolate aspect becomes appalling from the moment the Greek Convent of Mar Saba is passed. For miles around the sea the soil has assumed a volcanic character, and neither a blade of grass nor a spray of lichen relieves the oppressed eye. The awful silence of the dismal environment is never broken by the song of birds or the gurgling of rills. All nature is wrapped in a black winding sheet. Low mounds of earth still mark the location of Sodom, and images of the doomed city, with its cursed inhabitants, unbidden, flit before the imagination.

Toward the end of January, a few years ago, our caravan reached the Dead Sea, and as the thermometer registered over ninety degrees Fahrenheit, many of us took a plunge in the salt and bitter waters of the huge caldron. Contrary to all expectation, we found the bath delightfully cool, and but for the fact that we could not sink, we might have believed ourselves at Boulogne or at Brighton.

I will relate one incident which those not accustomed to horseback riding will do well to remember, if ever they go there. We had ridden our horses during seven consecutive hours before reaching the water, and one of us, not prepared for such a long ride, was naturally feeling its unpleasant effects. Ignorant of his incapability of enjoying the peculiar properties of salt under such circumstances, our friend dropped, lamb-like, into the sea. It were superfluous to add that he displayed due haste in returning ashore. Had he sat down upon a bunch of prickly pears, no greater want of composure could have been expected.

On our way to the river Jordan we felt a disagreeable sensation from the clammy and salty matter which the evaporation of the water had left upon our skin. One hour after leaving the arid shores of the sea we were all made happy by washing off this greasy substance in the *Eshsheriah, i. e.*, "the watering-place."

The appearance of the much vaunted Jordan either must have undergone an astonishing metamorphosis, or its beauty has only existed in the minds of enthusiastic narrators. Whatever the explanation, this most celebrated among rivers is to-day only a narrow and rapid stream of turbid water, with an uninteresting flora lining its muddy banks.

IX.

Russia needs a foothold upon the shores of the Mediterranean, and when the Bear is ready we may expect to see him pounce

---
*Arabic name for the river Jordan.

upon Joppa. The Jews must not entertain the hope of regaining possession of Jerusalem during these times, because Asia Minor will be for many years to come in the hands of their avowed enemies, the Turks or the Russians.

Some American and English utopists dream of colonizing the Holy Land, developing its resources, Christianizing the Arabs, rebuilding Jerusalem, and so forth. If these men be possessed of the least patriotism they would better turn their attention to the fertile and uncultivated plains of the great West, or to the undeveloped colonies of the British Empire. The advantages possible in many cities and regions over those of Jerusalem and Palestine, are obvious to minds free from fanaticism. That sincere Mohammedans can not be Christianized has often been proved, and that hypocrites can not be benefitted by a change of mask is self-evident. Let the efforts of our missionaries be stored for home consumption. This desire to civilize the Arabs may be wholly unselfish on the part of these men, for it is hardly probable that they intend to practise the subtle English art of fastening commercial fetters on unsophisticated natives under the pretense of spreading the gospel. These dreamers' veneration for the holy places may be noble, but a modern crusade, in this age of enlightenment, however venerable its object, however humane its course, would only entitle its projectors to the derision of the world.

The splendor of Jerusalem, and the thrilling phases in her history, were born of a spirit differing vastly from the one towards which mankind is advancing. To-day men are actuated by utility, not by faith. The torch of progress lights their way to nobler deeds than are recorded in the annals of the Land of Canaan. The vicissitudes of Jerusalem were the outcome of religious dissensions, and, from the nature of things, the future history of Solomon's capital will be less interesting than the past has been, because conflicts must diminish in frequency and intensity as man approaches Civilization and her fair daughter Toleration.

CHAPTER X.

FROM CONSTANTINOPLE TO VIENNA.

I.

At the mouth of the Golden Horn, the placid and picturesque harbor of Stamboul (Constantinople), that most interesting city :
"By Pontus' mouth upon the shore of Thrace,"
we lifted our anchor one mild February day, and steamed away into the Bosphorus, the renowned strait which unites the Black Sea with the Sea of Marmora and divides Asia from Europe. The average temperature of the water was like that of the air, and this was as in summer. The climate of Constantinople is usually temperate, even during the winter months. The Bosphorus was frozen only six times since the eighth century A. D.

I was on my way to Vienna via the

Oriental Express, which awaited our steamer at the Bulgarian seaport of Varna, ninety miles away. The proprietor of the hotel in Constantinople had warned me not to go by that route before April. He described graphically the sufferings of some travelers who had just arrived from the Danube. Thinking he was stressing unduly upon these hardships to contrast them more effectively with the comforts of his house, I decided to follow my own inclinations, and I secured a berth upon the German Lloyd steamer which was to carry me to the railway station in Varna. If ever again I meet that landlord I shall apologize for my skepticism.

The scenery along the entire Bosphorus is indescribably beautiful. Nature and art have wedded to bring forth an earthly paradise. I cannot attempt to describe the marvelous panorama which dazzles the tourist who sails over this magic water-way. The mere recollection of the varied and charming scenes I beheld from the steamer, transports me into a sweet reverie and confuses my hapless pen by the multiplicity, complexity, and splendor of the mental images it evokes. Along the north shore of the Golden Horn, Galata spreads out. This quarter of the city rises to the crest of the hill, and is crowned by a massive tower. Beyond and above Galata, Pera unfolds itself parallel with the shore. In Galata many Christians dwell; Pera is the seat of the diplomatic body. The larger part of Constantinople, with its forest of minarets, its numberless mosques, including the celebrated St. Sophia, and with the luxuriant gardens and graceful buildings of the Sultan's seraglio, is situated on the south shore. On the right, across the narrow Bosphorus, expands Scutari—the *Père la Chaise* of Stamboul—a sad and solemn city of tombs, with its rows of cypresses so suggestive of tears.

II.

While the temperature may be warm and the weather fine upon the Bosphorus, it often happens that just beyond its mouth, in the Black Sea, a tempest is raging. Black Sea! I shudder at the mention of that name, and with reason. The Black Sea, the *Pontus Euxinus* of the ancients, is bounded on the west by the Turkish provinces of Rumilia, Bulgaria, and Moldavia; on the north by South Russia; on the east by the Russian provinces of Circassia and Transcaucasia; and on the south by the Turkish provinces of Asia Minor. It is entered from the Mediterranean by the Dardanelles, the Sea of Marmora and the Bosphorus. The Greek navigators who first sailed over it were repulsed or massacred by some of the tribes inhabiting its coasts. Thus their countrymen named it the "sea unfriendly to strangers," (*Pontus Axenos.*) Later, having established colonies along its shores, they changed the name to *Euxinus*, (friendly.) The modern name was given it by the Turks, who found this sea, as I did to my ineffable discomfort, subject to sudden and violent storms, to a very variable temperature, and to thick fogs. I can convince any one that the epithet "black" is not a misnomer for this treacherous body of water, tempest-torn by warring, chilling winds, which, uninterrupted by high mountain ranges, sweep down from the Arctic regions blowing over the snow-filled and ice-bound steppes of Russia. The northern shores are often blockaded with ice during the winter, especially where the water is shallow, and contains less salt, as at the entrance of rivers. This sea is noted for the rapidity with which frightful storms arise, often to subside again as rapidly. I did not know of these ugly characteristics, or I would not have left Constantinople, at least, by that road.

Had I had the slightest intimation of what the Black Sea had in store for me, I would rather have forsaken fortune, home, friends, country, and even embraced the faith of Mohammed with its worldly ethics. Now I might be exclaiming from the top of some white and slender minaret: "*Lâ ilâha ill' Allâh, wa Muhammedu-rrasul-Allâh*, ("There is no God but Allah, and Mohammed is His prophet.") Who knows?

III.

The Bosphorus was so calm that, when evening came, I could not remember having felt the motion of our little steamer. The air was so balmy, and the afternoon had passed away so dreamily in the charms of the present and the blissful ignorance of the future! At six, just as we reached the lighthouse at the end of the Bosphorus, the captain brought our ship to a dead stop, and invited us to the dining-room where dinner was served. During that meal many passengers complained about stopping for dinner. Almost every one agreed that the captain was a fool to make us lose that time. Now, I bless that captain. Without his precaution, I would have had to seek on the ceiling the olives and caviar, served as first *hors d' œuvres*, supposing that I should have retained the least vestige of an appetite while the ship was up-side down.

At the table, I met an accomplished and pretty little woman, the Baroness Blanc, *née* Terry, of New York, whose husband was Italian Ambassador to Turkey; now he is a member of the Italian Cabinet.

The food and wines were good, the company agreeable, and an hour was spent delightfully. See the reverse of the medal. We had relished our meal. Brrrr!! when I think of it! At about seven o'clock we were drowsily sipping some brandy and coffee from tiny Turkish cups when the factotum, our captain, again said something which added markedly to his unpopularity. "Ladies and gentlemen," said he, with a sardonic smile, "I would advise you to go to your berths; we are about to start."

"Does he think we are children?" indignantly exclaimed a handsome English blonde.

"I shall report the conduct of this impudent fellow at the Vienna office!" added a military-looking Austrian. Other similar expressions of annoyance, disgust, contempt, and hate, were applied to this naval busybody, and from one end of the table to the other, *sotto voce*, anathemas in Asiatic and European tongues were hurled at him.

Of course, very few passengers followed the captain's advice, which I characterized as arrogant and useless. Now, I think it was practical and benign. I had stubbornly placed myself near the stove, with the intention of staying away from my berth as long as I wanted, captain or no captain. At precisely a quarter after seven, the order to steam away rang above, and two minutes after, I was making a diagonal bee-line for the other end of the dining-room. I cannot remember where I landed, either objectively or subjectively. One thing I knew, we had just entered the seething, foaming, furious, tempestuous Black Sea.

IV.

From that memorable moment, and for thirty-six mortal hours, (I was about to write, centuries,) our ship was shaken by the waves as a rat-terrier would shake a mouse; the difference in our case being that there was no intermission to the frightful turbulence. Now we would feel a slight tremor, then a jar, a quiver, and again for the millionth time a monstrous wave would strike the deck as if to crush it into atoms. Each of those billows seemed to weigh a hundred tons, and as it struck our deck it sounded like the explosion of a dynamite factory. During the oscillations of our steamer, caused by the terrible blows from these water claw-hammers, the wood-work would crack as if to break asunder. The pandemonium caused by the unchained elements was not all that split our aching ears. In addition, I had to listen to these wailings from children and women: "Oh! Heaven! we'll never see home again. "Ma! Ah! I am so sick!" "George! George! Alas! Why did we ever leave mother?" "Captain, will we ever reach Varna? Hee! Hee!!"

Thus, for thirty-six hours, while I clung to the bench, which, fortunately, was made fast to the partition, I endured the whole catalogue of physical and mental pains: thirst, hunger, cold, headache, nausea, fatigue, despair, disgust, anger, remorse, fear, and . . . . several others. I reviewed my past, and felt disappointed at its worthlessness. But there is an end to everything and, more dead than alive, I reached the coast of Bulgaria.

The day before we were breathing in the soft clime of the East, in the land of the sun ; now, we shivered under our thickest winter clothing. The rigging of our ship was one mass of icicles and the deck was covered with ten inches of snow. It is fortunate that we were not out much longer, for I do not think I could have lived another day under such horrible circumstances. A tall and strong Englishman, a dear old friend of mine, gently tucked me under his overcoat and carried me like a valise to our railway carriage, which stood but a few rods from the landing.

"How frozen and how faint I then became
"Ask me not, reader! for I write it not
"Since words would fail to tell thee of my state.
"I was not dead nor living."

And this was the result of what is called *pleasure* travel.

The stormy blast of hell with restless fury cannot be worse than the Black Sea. The only difference is one of taste: it is between burning and freezing. In so far as the other varieties of agony which these two places offer, or are supposed to offer, there is but small choice. Had I to decide between these two realms of sorrow, I think I would select the unexplored one—first, because I am so fond of traveling; second, because until the last moment I could enjoy my doubts about the tortures of the other place, while I am convinced of the malignity of the Black Sea.

v.

We traveled by rail all that night, and arrived in the dismal city of Rustchuk at the other end of Bulgaria—the most forlorn country I have ever traversed, not excepting Canada.

Along the coast there are many mongrel types called Gagaous. The real Bulgarians look down upon them, I am told, and I fail to see why. It is the chimney-sweep scorning the scavenger. The Bulgarians sprang from the Finnish. Like their ancestors, they have light, thin hair; eyelids half open; high cheek bones; the face is frequently oval, the complexion coarse, the expression harsh, and their manners are anything but elegant. Their unmusical language is fundamentally Slavonic and mixed with Turkish and Persian. Although it contains a considerable amount of Greek and Latin, I was not able to understand one word while in that dreary land.

After resting one day and one night in a miserable hovel, the leading hotel of Rustchuk—hear that mellifluous name!—I started to cross the Danube, whose " beautiful blue " had turned into a cheerless gray, perhaps for my especial delectation. Large lumps of ice here, and an uneven frozen surface there, extended over the river for two or three hundred yards. Had it reached the opposite bank it would not have been so unpleasant. We could have crossed on foot in a straight line, and saved much time while avoiding further discomfort. As it was, we had to walk on the ice until the water's edge, then take a canoe to reach the next frozen point. After walking again over the slippery way we had to bargain with dishonest boatmen who, knowing our predicament, took advantage of us, and charged exhorbitant fees to carry us beyond. With the temperature below zero, we changed boats four times and walked uninterruptedly over the ice for five hours to cross this "beautiful blue" Danube.

In Bucharest, Roumania, I found the best hotel I had seen since leaving Naples for the Orient, some months before.

It is possible that the hostelry seemed better than it was on account of the inconveniences I had suffered in Bedouin tents, Egyptian Khans, and Greek inns. The manager of this pretty, though small, establishment was formerly the king's cook. Some wealthy Roumanians induced him to give up the royal appointment, that they might have a sort of club-house where Parisian dinners could be had. The gilded youths of Roumania are generally educated in Paris; they speak French, and cultivate French tastes. Bucharest is a lovely city. One is startled to find such grace and refinement so far from the beaten paths of travel.

From Bucharest I went to Buda-Pesth, where I saw a splendid performance of Verdi's "Othello." Thence I left for Vienna, reaching the gay Austrian capital, the other Paris of the world, in time to attend the performance of Goldmark's

"Queen of Sheba," at the Royal Opera House, under the direction of Goldmark himself. The *ensemble* was perfect. After the opera in Paris, that in Vienna satisfies most. Neither Milan nor Dresden can answer so fully the demands of the fastidious auditor.

CHAPTER XI.

INCIDENTS EN VOYAGE.

I.

I had bought a large and handsome trunk just before leaving Paris for Switzerland. It was covered with glistening brass buttons and steel corner pieces. A magnificent strap encircled it. Immediately after purchasing it I became sorry. It was so large! I had absolutely no use for it, having already two other trunks. However, I had to take it along. At the time, I did not dream that this unwise purchase could be turned to good account. Next morning I arrived in Geneva. Having slept in an easy chair through the night I must have looked haggard and worn. First-class carriages in most European trains contain no lavatories, and my face and hands were soiled with cinders and dust. My slouch hat and wrinkled coat added to my disreputable appearance. As I approached the hotel, its manager came to greet me upon the steps. Said I in English: "I would like to get a room fronting the lake." Instead of answering, he looked me over with a suspecting eye and hesitated. Quicker than it takes to write it, I surmised the cause of this cold reception. My disarranged clothing and generally careless appearance had led him to conclude I was not a desirable guest for the first hotel in Geneva. But my trunk had not been purchased in vain. It gave me character. The porter who had handled the voluminous Saratoga—my only passport—understood the situation at once, and exclaimed from the top of the omnibus:—

"*Monsieur est très comme il faut,*" while waving his hand, as much as to say: "He's all right."

Then there was no end of salutations,

and I was ushered into the best room facing the lake.

II.

On the Continent it is not customary to go to *table d'hôte* in full dress. Many Americans do not know this. At the Grand Hôtel in Naples at dinner, was seated on my right Princess Margherita, next to her her husband. Facing me, were two persons dressed, to use a colloquialism, "to kill." The woman wore a *decoletté* gown, probably made by Worth; he was in dress suit that fitted him like a glove. Both were bedecked with jewels. In marked contrast the Prince and Princess wore their everyday clothes, and these were of the most modest fashion. English was the language spoken by all at the table, as is often the case in first-class hotels on the Continent. The natives who travel in their own country, do not usually go to the best hotels. It would be quite safe to speak Italian at a hotel of this character, without fearing to be understood. The Princess, not believing I could understand her, as I had been speaking English to some ladies on my left, whispered to her husband in Italian:

"Prince, who is this noble Lord with his Lady facing us?"

The Prince answered: "I recollect having seen him while visiting the United States; he is a codfish merchant."

"Well," retorted the Princess, "you know, dear, how I dislike codfish. Now I shall surely hate it."

III.

With two English friends we had decided to visit Corinth. It was necessary to hire a carriage and a courier, in order to do so, from Athens, where we were. Our landlord, from whom I had asked information in relation to that trip, sent a courier to my room, who said to me:

"I will furnish the conveyance, the food, the wines, and guide you and these two gentlemen for one hundred francs a day each, and," he added in an undertone close to my ear, "the one hundred francs I will charge for you, you can put in your own pocket,—see?"

He had taken me for the courier of my friends. The fellow felt quite abashed when I told him we would accept his terms of two hundred francs a day for the three, but that I would pay my own share as I was not a courier.

IV.

I had an experience almost similar to this in Paris a few months after. Some lady friends from Brooklyn had asked me to secure a box for them at the Grand Opera. We went together to one of the stores facing the opera house, where theatre seats and boxes are sold. The clerk had heard me speak English with these ladies and had seen them hand me their pocketbook from which to pay for their box. When I inquired the price of the box he answered: "One hundred and sixty francs." Then he softly said to me:

"The sixty francs, you know, are for you."

This time I did not wish to humiliat the fellow, but wanting to carry the joke further I said to him in French:

"Please give me a receipt for the one hundred and sixty francs, because I have to account for everything I pay out."

I counted out to him the one hundred and sixty francs, got my receipt, and as I was leaving the store, he slyly handed me sixty francs in gold and said:

"I hope you will bring us many more of these pigeons."

My friends were astounded when I gave them back their sixty francs and told them how near they came to being plumed. It is needless to say I had again been taken for one of those dishonest couriers who receive a daily fee for showing you the sights and who yet exploit you at every step.

V.

The Hungarians hate the Austrians. They will not even speak German, though able to do so. One day I lost my way in Buda-Pesth, and I asked an intelligent looking fellow in German :

"Where is the Grand Hotel?"

He looked at me scornfully and exclaimed something angrily in Hungarian. I did not understand the words, but from his physiognomy, the shrugging of his shoulders, and the modulation of his voice, I drew the inference that he meant:
"I will not tell you."

And I was quite right. Upon returning to the hotel I told this to the proprietor, who said to me:

"The fellow understood you very well.

He was a Hungarian, and, taking you for a German, disdained to answer you."

VI.

On my way to Naples in the same railway compartment was a well-known American sculptor and wife, who, by the way, was old enough to be his mother-in-law. She stepped out of the carriage at a station to see if there was a good dining-room, and finding a satisfactory one, she beckoned to her husband. A man in our compartment, thinking that our sculptor had not seen the lady's motions, said to him :

"Pardon me, sir ; but your mother is beckoning to you."

"The lady is my wife, sir !" retorted the artist, in a tone that in itself told volumes.

Tableau !

VII.

Walking about the streets of Bologna,

I met an intelligent boy of twenty whom I asked to show me the way to the university. He, too, was going there, said he, as he was a student. We had not chatted long before he knew that I came from America. Learning this, he asked:

"Do you know my brother? His name is Giovanni Salvatore."

"Well," said I, "I don't know. Where does he live?"

"He is in Montevideo."

"No," answered I, which disappointed him greatly.

VIII.

This is not an unusual occurrence in Europe. The ignorance concerning America and American things is at times appalling. I remember a well-educated man who was astonished when I told him that Chicago was not in Harlem. He thought it was one of the suburbs of New York. Of course he did not intend to joke about the Windy City, but my information caused him to give up the intention of visiting the Exposition. Europeans should not be expected to know as much about America as Americans should know about Europe, for, no doubt, there is more on the other side that should be known. What do we Americans, for example, know of India, of Australia, and even of South America? However, I think that Europeans could benefit greatly by studying our country and, particularly, by copying our business systems. It is heart-rending to any one accustomed to the rapid way in which commercial transactions are carried on here, to find himself obliged to go through the red tape of Europe for the simplest affairs.

IX.

Having been in the United States only a few days and not having studied English before coming to America, I knew but a few words of that language. At a hotel table a woman seated near me asked me :

"Are you hungry to-day?"

"No, madam," answered I, with the proudest air I could assume, "I am French."

"*Hongrois*," in French means Hungarian. I misunderstood her question and thought it referred to my nationality. Those who heard me, of course, smiled ; some even laughed. Had I appreciated the cause of the merriment, I, too, would have enjoyed the situation, though at my expense. At that moment, however, my national pride was wounded, for I thought these horrid Americans had insulted my nation by their laughter. Could I have been able to express myself in English, I would have told them volumes about Gaul's greatness, about Charlemagne, about Napoleon.

Luckily I found no words for utterance,

though I was bursting with stirred feelings and burning thoughts. Two weeks later, while studying English, I chanced upon the verb "to be hungry." This was the key to my recent dilemma, and then, even at that late hour I, too, laughed heartily.

X.

About that time, while I was at a desk writing, some one asked to borrow my pen-holder. I immediately passed the rack which held the pen-holders. My interlocutor smiled and said: "This is not a pen-holder." But I could not see why until he explained, for to me it was evident that this rack was "holding" pens, and therefore was a "pen-holder." This conclusion was certainly not wholly illogical. When guessing at the meaning of words or phrases, one is often deceived; while some analogies in sound, etymology, or construction may help the guesser, they also often lead him to incorrect deductions.

XI.

Guides, hotel servants, and others, whose employment brings them in contact with the traveling public in Europe, are acquainted with the language of tourists only to the extent of the limited vocabulary essential in the pursuit of their occupations. Ask a *cicerone* whose life is spent guiding visitors through one cathedral: "What comes after the salad?" and he will probably answer, "Noddin', dees catedral is all." On the other hand, if you say to your waiter: "What is the most important building in town?" he will be quite apt to reply: "*Omelette au rhum.*"

In Lyons, while dining with some American acquaintances, we decided to go to the theatre that evening. We had just finished the soup. Turning to the waiter, I said in English: "What is the best entertainment we can go to this evening?" "Salmon," answered he, thinking I had asked about the next course.

XII.

A young woman, who was not blessed with the knowledge of her own ignorance, was boasting that she understood Italian perfectly. Some one asked her to translate the sentence, *"Quell' amore, quell' affeto."* (This love, this affection.) And she, guided by the similarity in sound and by her unbounded presumption, promptly answered:

"Why, this is easy enough. It means 'quell your love, quell your affection."

XIII.

I had been in Germany less than a month. One day, in Nüremberg, I decided to take an early train next morning. Calling the porter of the hotel, I said in the purest Hanoverian accent I could command:

"Portier, Morgen muss ich um fünf 'wachsen.'"

Which meant "To-morrow at five I must 'grow.'" I had intended to say, *'erwachen'*, (wake up) instead of grow. As my stature is very short, the reader can imagine how ludicrous my remark sounded.

After reaching my room, the intended verb came to me, and I looked over the balustrade to note the effect of my error. Down stairs I saw eight or ten men convulsed with laughter, while the porter was referring to my height by holding the flat of his hand about three feet above the floor, and remarking: "Of course, he should grow."

XIV.

An American girl asked a German doctor, "What do you think of my German?" "Mees," he retorted, "I ding you speek peutifully—and I am not *flirting*," (flattering.)

XV.

In Philadelphia I had lost my way. I asked a foreigner who happened to be passing: "Where is Chestnut street, please?" Thinking I wanted to know the hour he pulled out his watch and said "Tree o'cloack an a 'alf."

XVI.

In French "*un peu*" means either "a little," or "a few." Should you ask a Frenchman if he speaks English, do not wonder if five times in ten he answers: "A few." Most English people pronounce the syllable "*eu*" as if it were written "oo." Thus "*un poo*" *(pou)* would sound in French like the name given to the small, white parasite scientifically known as the "*pediculus capitis.*" The majority of Americans, when asked if they speak French, usually answer: "*Un pou.*" The apprehension of the effect this produces upon the ear of a Frenchman is left to the imagination of the reader.

XVII.

With some German artists I had attended a concert given for the benefit of patients at a prominent hospital for the insane. The superintendent invited us to a little luncheon after the performance. German was the language of the occasion. I was then beginning my studies in that tongue. It is a rule that those who know the least about a thing are most anxious to display their little knowledge. During the luncheon I seized an opportunity that will prove this rule. Every one at the table had said something, but I had been silent, not being able to recall a sentence, however short, that might be regarded as pertinent. Suddenly, as an inspiration, something came to me that I regarded as most fitting. I had just concluded eating, and wishing to excuse myself from the table, I calmly said, "*Entschuldigen sie mich meine Herren, ich bin 'verrückt'.*" ("Excuse me, gentlemen, I am 'crazy.'") "*Vertig*," (finished) was the word I should have used. The superintendent very politely and without so much as a smile upon his lips, expressed the greatest solicitude for me, and offered to reserve a good room. Then he explained to me my mistake. It goes without saying that much fun was had out of this slip of my tongue.

CHAPTER XII.

HAPPINESS VERSUS TRAVEL.

"Fixed to no spot is happiness sincere,
'Tis nowhere to be found, or any where."

On a pleasure tour through Europe and the Orient, if one have the power to cast aside all business and social preoccupations, and that sure destroyer of human blessings—ambition—it becomes quite possible to reach a state akin to contentment, if not to happiness. Abroad, the active American breathes the balmy air of a quiet art-life, something new and re-creating to him. Travel, notwithstanding its worries and discomforts, affords him a more refined existence than the hum-drum of the daily routine at home. If far from the bee-hive called America, no ominous commercial cloud appears to darken his sky, he may revel, undisturbed, in many tangible pleasures, and in the charms of his imagination, sensations and and perceptions unknown to him in the vortex of his transatlantic affairs. Of course he must give up the eternal hope of augmenting his material possessions; in fact he has to diminish them with good grace. As a compensation, he may gather in his mental coffers a treasure more precious than gold: the knowledge of human nature. This, with the realization of his own insignificance and the true appreciation of the narrowness of his world of action, may serve to make his future intellectual life of more value to himself and fellow men. He will thus be better prepared to recognize the truth, whatever be its cloak.

Vivid pleasures are not found in the whirl of travel. Though amidst changing scenes, one feels satisfied, not joyous. The days flow placidly in the contemplation of dream-like realities. You drink copiously in the beautifully-wrought wisdom-cup which Dame Nature daintily serves. Going from country to country, while observing at every hour some new and striking fact, quenches the thirst for knowledge with an invigorating beverage. Some travel merely that they may be able to say they have traveled; others, more serious, do so that they may read many pages in the infinite book of life. And these students cannot see much without remembering much; there could be for them no deeper fountain of learning. Men, in the boundless fields of their endeavours, and with their strongly-contrasted racial and national traits, appear to the bewildered tourist as if moving in a vast kaleidoscope. The art, the literature, the politics, the ethics, and the commerce of other nations, all become potent teachers. The more uncommon the precept, and the more eccentric the example, the deeper the impression.

In his wildest imaginings, no novelist

could invent that which may be observed almost at every step. These dissolving views, reproduced from nature, at times are so odd, outlandish, wonderful, as to seem indeed stranger than fiction. Yet it is the same human heart and the same Mother Earth, though aspects may be ever so varied.

II.

Can one find happiness in these peregrinations? He who seeks it there is a fool or a child. 'Tis the rainbow in the ever-receding horizon which baby fingers would touch. No! There cannot be bliss even for the most favored of travelers; what would have been the use of inventing a paradise if it could be found on earth? Chamfort said it was difficult to find happiness in ourselves, and impossible elsewhere. Schopenhauer, the philosopher who has seen the world, wrote that it consisted in undisturbed leisure and great intellect, with freedom from pain and boredom. To Aristotle happiness consisted in leisure. I am quite content if I can enter merely the peristyle of the Temple of Felicity, through the opportunities for travel, equanimity of temper, the possession of liberty, competence, health, education, the friendship of a few equals, and the power to borrow no trouble and to disdain the inevitable. Moral philosophers will say that I am worldly; that not wealth, or health, or travel is the basis of happiness ; that animal sensations should be divorced from the pleasures of the soul, which, alone, in its peace and harmony, can give men blessedness ; that happiness is the glorious triumph of mind over matter, and that the primary step to mundane beatitude is the control of the appetites and passions.

But I cannot live at such an elevation; its rarefied air would stifle me, and I fear it might stop the breath even of my gentle reader. Life would not be worth living without our small vices, and the love of sight-seeing is a universal one.

Socrates praised leisure as the fairest of all possessions. Yet, with this do nothing there comes a serious obstacle to happiness. "It is so difficult to keep quiet when one has nothing to do." The result is that you begin to travel in quest of keen pleasures, and, instead, you find but mild amusements after much labor, sometimes amounting to hardship. Upon returning home you begin to think it were preferable not to have gone. Having enjoyed better things than your own country affords, it becomes difficult to relish existence there again for a prolonged period. You have acquired tastes which cannot be gratified simultaneously anywhere. You feel *blasé*, almost disgusted with life itself. Work, the universal panacea, is inefficacious against your melancholy. Then you conclude it was folly that impelled you far from your birthplace in quest of ephemeral pleasures which were to be accompanied by so many regrets. After frequent inconveniences and dangers you go back to your former companions and haunts disillusioned and discontented, though wiser. The reminiscences of the pleasant moments you have passed among strange things and men at times delight you, but more frequently, like sea-sickness after a good repast, they come to nauseate the stomach of your memory.

If happiness be the true end of life, notwithstanding the knowledge gained, and the pleasure felt in traveling, you decide it were better not to have left your native land.

THE END.

ELLA WHEELER WILCOX'S PREFACE TO THE FIRST EDITION OF "OBSERVATIONS OF A MUSICIAN," BY LOUIS LOMBARD.

Louis Lombard is the great grandson of a French Roman Catholic Bishop, who married during the revolution of 1793 in order to escape the guillotine. His maternal ancestors were an influential Italian family.

He was born in Lyons, France, Dec. 15, 1861. At the age of ten he was admitted to the classes of violin, solfeggio, and harmony in the National Conservatory of Music of Marseilles. A concert tour of two years was the occasion of his first visit to America, after which he returned to Paris to prosecute his studies. Returning to this country, he became identified with our musical interests.

The public at this time caught a glimpse of his composition in the music of a comic opera.

In 1887 he again went abroad, traveling through Europe, Asia, and Africa, his proficiency in six languages enabling him to secure most interesting and valuable information, which he utilized in the leading magazines of the country.

Upon his return, a desire for practical insight into the management of business affairs led him to enter the Columbia Law School of New York. Uniting this experience with that which his well-directed life had given him, he, in 1889, opened the Conservatory of Music in Utica, New York, with a strong financial guarantee from one hundred prominent citizens of the place, six professors, and one hundred and ninety-six students. To-day, that institution, modeled closely after the Paris Conservatory, is second to none in the United States, in all that goes to make the genuine musician. It has a faculty of fifteen of the ablest European and American teachers, and four hundred pupils in attendance from all parts of the States and Canada.

It is difficult to imagine how so much talent, knowledge, energy, executive ability, and soul, can be encompassed in so small a body. Louis Lombard, though well-proportioned, is but five feet one inch in height. The elegance of his manner, combined with those other talents rarely found in one so devoted to art, have won him many friends and a bountiful success, which has not yet reached half its fulness. Last summer he was unanimously elected chairman of the executive committee of the Music Teachers' National Association.

Louis Lombard is now recognised not only as an educator, conductor, violinist, composer, critic, but also as a writer of rare ability, having a peculiar talent of securing an involuntary following of a true and pure classical standard, through a modern attractiveness that is irresistible.

A better illustration of this cannot be

given than by referring to his articles recently published in New York magazines.

In commending this volume upon musical topics, I am but doing the cause of music, no less than its distinguished representative, simple justice. I do it most sincerely.

New York, March 15, 1893.

READ

OBSERVATIONS
OF A
MUSICIAN.

BY

LOUIS LOMBARD.

Second Edition, Augmented.

⁎ *Will be sent, bound in cloth, postpaid, upon receipt of 50 cents in stamps, money-order, or currency. Address,*

Utica Conservatory of Music,
UTICA, N. Y.

UNSOLICITED LETTERS.

Taken from Among Hundreds of Flattering Communications Written by Eminent Men and Women in Relation to the

FIRST EDITION OF
Observations of a Musician.
BY LOUIS LOMBARD.

CARL FAELTEN, Director, New England Conservatory of Music: Boston, March 25, '93.—I have read your "Observations" with great interest, and I find, especially your various essays on musical education, most excellently written. I am always happy to find one more who has the courage to express his opinion whether people may like it or not.

ROSE ELIZABETH CLEVELAND: "The Weeds," Holland Patent, N. Y., Aug. 5, '93.—Your charming and valuable booklet has enough good reading in it for a much larger work. However, it is wiser to condense as you have.

FRANCES F. CLEVELAND: Executive Mansion, Washington, March 23, '93.—"Observations of a Musician" will be carefully preserved.

W. S. B. MATHEWS, Composer, Critic, Writer, and Editor of "Music:" Chicago, March 24, '93. —I would like to reprint some of the essays from your charming little book, say that on Spanish

Music. You have done these things extremely well. Your style and matter are both so elegant and so sensible withal, that it is a great pleasure to read them. I think an essay in "Music" now and then would forward your recognition in the country at large as a writer of rare powers.

The REV. OREN ROOT, Professor of Mathematics, Hamilton College: Clinton, N. Y., April 12, 93,—The "Observations of a Musician" have a deal of most admirable sense and most practical sentiment. My experience as a teacher, running over five and thirty years, indorses your suggestions, and my observations as a clergyman emphasize them again.

PETER RUDOLPH NEFF, President, College of Music: Cincinnati, April 14, '93.—I have read the "Observations" with much interest. Judicious views, the result of unusual opportunities for observation, clothed in charming diction, and the book is one of the few which few hold the attention of the reader until he reaches "The end."

EVERETT SMITH, Mayor of Schenectady, N. Y.: March 30, '93.—The thoughts contained in "Observations of a Musician" appeal strongly to one's good sense. It is a work which should be a textbook, and I sincerely hope that you may permit more than the one edition to be issued.

F. TOLEDO, Artistic Director, the Æolian Organ Co.: New York, Nov, 2, '93.—In your 114 pages you say more than others do in hundreds and hundreds.

The REV. CLARENCE E. RICE, School Director: Tokio, Japan, April 25, '93.—I am impressed with the feeling that your book is practical and deals with problems from a side that musicians have not generally the talent to present. The book will do good.

G. B. POLLERI, one of the leading Musical Composers in Italy: Genoa, Italy, April 6, '93.—I have read the "Observations" with great pleasure. They are exquisite in substance and form. It is a style which can be read only with pleasure; it is one that invites the reader. How many truths in your book! and not alone applicable to America, but to all countries.

I. V. FLAGLER, the Chautauqua Lecturer and Organist: Auburn, N. Y., March 28, '93.—It is both entertaining and instructive, and should be read, not only by every musician and musical student, but by every one. Its sale should not be limited to 1,000, but should exceed 1,000,000.

ED. SCHUBERTH, the prominent Musical Publisher: New York City, March 24, '93.—A very interesting book.

MRS. F. M. LATHROP: New York city, March 27, '93.—The little book is attractive and will, I think, do some good work in the field for which it has been created. It is a little missionary sent out with no parade of society, but it will find its way quite as well into all the nooks and crannies of heathendom.

SENATOR H. J. COGGESHALL: Albany, N. Y., April 3, '93.—I prize the book highly.

CHARLES DANCLA, Knight of the Legion of Honor, and Professor at the Conservatory: Paris, France, April 29, '93.—You, who speak all languages, you will read more easily the little book I send you, than I could read yours, which was translated to me by one who understands English. Your book has interested me greatly.

PAUL ROCHE, Professor at the Conservatory: Marseilles, France, April 11, '93.—In this interesting book you have displayed a talent as littérateur which I did not know you possessed. Bravo! That is a splendid work. I was agreeably surprised. Your travels have borne fruit.

FEDERIGO BARGILE, Canon of the Cathedral: Fiesole, Italy, April 23, '93.-After reading your book over and over, I take pleasure in telling you that I regard it as a work full of sense, of just musical criticisms, and rich and sound judgment regarding music everywhere. It is written in an unaffected style, and it is very readable. I congratulate you. I confess it is an additional proof of your great talent for the beautiful art which you profess, and of the fine genius with which nature has so courteously endowed you.

FANNIE EDGAR THOMAS, the well known Critic and Writer: New York, May 2, '93.—I am truly delighted with your charming little book, holding, packed, so many gems of musical truth. How true that it was the echo of my thought on each topic. Not alone that, but the truths are stated in a manner to compel the conviction of every reader, whether a thinker or not. And that is why I feel so relieved after reading the book. I had an idea of culling some of the fat epigrams as mottoes for my articles, but would feel obliged to take the thing entire. So many of the ideas have been partially or clumsily expressed in my hearing, that I should imagine the book would have a large reading amongst thinking musicians. I have read over and over again your "Music for the People," first with the gluttonous curiosity I always feel as to what point you will make, and again to enjoy seeing *how* you do that. To one who knows your mind, it is even more masterful, than to the mind uneducated in your art of thought, It is so subtly simple, logical, to the very door of conviction, airily popular in its over-current, and rigorously musical in its under-current. Good art that!

MRS. J. MAURY PATTEN: Washington, D. C., Oct. 15, '93.—While spending an evening with Mrs. ———, I chanced upon your "Observations of a Musician," and was so pleased with the book that upon my return home I bought a copy. I thank you for having put into print such delightful essays, and ones of such usefulness to the real earnest student and a lover of music.

ZÉLIE DE LUSSAN, the celebrated Prima-Donna: London, England, Aug. 6, '93.—I have read your charming little book, and I thank you a thousand times. I need not tell you that I find it admirably written; in a word, as we say in English, "It is to the point." Let us hope that it will not be the last.

ALEXANDRE GUILMANT, the greatest living Organist and Composer of Music for the Organ : Paris, France, October, '93. I have just read your magnificent article, and I do not know how to thank you. I have rarely read the appreciation of an artist written so well and with so just and exalted a sentiment in musical art. I have met many persons who admire your writings, and the Reverend Father Barry has read an extract from your pen to-day from the pulpit. Thanks, then, thousand and thousand times, and believe in my affectionate sentiments.

COUNT OF DOUVILLE-MAILLEFEU, Deputé: Paris, France, May 1, '93.—You write remarkably well.

DUDLEY BUCK, the best American Composer: Brooklyn, N. Y., October, '93.—You have a facile pen. I like your writings.

EDITORIAL NOTICES
of the
FIRST EDITION OF
OBSERVATIONS OF A MUSICIAN.
By LOUIS LOMBARD.

London and New York Review of Reviews, May, '93: Lombard's brief essays upon varied topics in the musical domain are most intelligent, pointed and up to date.

Chicago Times, July 15, '93: Written by one who is thoroughly familiar with all of which he speaks. The range of the essays is considerable, including criticism of music and musicians in many different countries. The criticisms are intelligent, fair and interesting. The author is already known in musical and other circles as a man of great talent, and this modest volume will indicate abilities in yet another direction.

Amsterdam (N. Y.) Democrat, March 20, '93: A series of bright, practical essays by Louis Lombard, the well-known educator, conductor, violinist, composer, critic and writer, the founder of the Utica Conservatory of Music. Full of valuable suggestions, especially to the young student, while the cultured musician will find much that is entertaining and helpful. Mr. Lombard is not only a thorough musician, but a keen critic, and his writings have always been sought for by the leading magazines. The preface is by Ella Wheeler Wilcox, who pays a graceful and deserved tribute to the writer. There is no doubt of the success of the work, and it is safe to predict a second edition in the near future.

Rochester (N. Y.) Herald, March 20, '93: A neat and valuable book. The "Observations" are of special value to musical students, but anybody can peruse them with entertainment and profit. Though a first-class artist, Louis Lombard is that rarety among artists, a practical man, and his advice and every-day philosophy are full of suggestion of merit. He has been an extensive traveler, and some of the chapters communicate the results of his observations abroad. Mr. Lombard is thoroughly imbued with American ideas, which he happily applies in his efforts to cultivate his art among the growing generation. His little volume is a gem in its way.

Utica (N. Y.) Herald, March 18, '93: A charming book from the pen of Louis Lombard, the versatile director of the Utica Conservatory. The preface is by Ella Wheeler Wilcox, who writes appreciatively of Mr. Lombard's talents and accomplishments. Of the Conservatory founded by him, she says: "Modeled closely after the Paris Conservatory, it is second to none in the U. S. in all that goes to make the genuine musician." The essays are eminently practical in their suggestiveness, and the bright style in which they are written of itself constitutes a charm. The cultured musician and the young student will both find them helpful and entertaining, while they will be of interest to all readers.

Chicago Music Review, Nov. '93: Musicians do now and then think, even in the popular definition of intellectual thought. Such a musician is Mr. Louis Lombard. The observations on "Why girls should play the Violin," and "Use and abuse of the Piano," are so good that I quote them entire. As an educationally suggestive little work it is to be commended to mothers especially, and also to students and teachers.

Rome (N. Y.) Sentinel, March 20, '93: An attractive volume which treats of much that entertains as well as instructs. Cannot fail to be interesting and valuable to a large class of people, and its success seems assured.

Saturday Globe, March 18, '93: Most interesting and instructive; promises to become a standard work on the subject of which it treats.

Utica (N. Y.) Press, March 18, '93: A very attractive book, interesting as well as instructive; will doubtless prove both valuable and popular and a large sale is predicted. The essays are well written and contain many suggestions of worth.

Albany (N. Y.) Sunday Press, March 19, '93: A compact, interesting, and instructive volume, useful alike to amateurs and professional musicians.

Chicago Presto, March 18, '93: While the work is of intense interest to the musical profession, it will also pay for a careful perusal by the general public.

Utica (N. Y.) Observer, March 22, '93: There are musicians and musicians, and the observations of one may obviously have greater value and interest than those of another. These are the utterances of the witty and original Prof. Louis Lombard, the head of the Utica Conservatory of Music. This makes a difference—a distinct difference when it is stated—in the way in which the "Observations" will be regarded. The volume takes hold on public interest here and wherever else he is known. Gifted as a musician and successful as a linguist, he is almost as remarkable as a writer. It is a book that will be prized, and will be taken up many times.

Binghamton (N. Y.) Democrat, March 20, '93: Replete with information of the art divine, from Jubal's time down.

Utica (N. Y.) Sunday Tribune, March 19, '93: One of the neatest little books. It consists of twenty-four essays on musical subjects, which are treated in Mr. Lombard's usual vigorous style.

Schenectady (N. Y.) Union, March 21, '93: Very readable and useful.

L'Eco d'Italia, of New York, March 23, '93: Un interessante libro. Vi sono in queste "Observations," capitoli molto interessanti e gli studii musicali sono trattati da un punto di vista nuovo ed originale. La esposizione e chiara e la dottrina molta.

New York Recorder, March 25, '93: Should interest artists.

Syracuse (N. Y.) Sunday Times, March 26, '93: Twenty-four chapters, tersely and ably penned, and covering a wide swath of musical culture. They are the honest observations of an accomplished musician who does not hesitate to tell the truth fearlessly. To the earnest student and unprejudiced teacher, Mr. Lombard's book will be a treasure.

Syracuse (N. Y.) News, March 27, '93: Cleverly written. Mr. Lombard tells many plain truths in a straightforward and practical manner. The book will be perused with interest.

Binghamton (N. Y.) Leader, March 22, '93: An entertaining and instructive brochure, not only interesting but valuable for the many useful suggestions it offers. It contains a wide range of topics within the scope of the musical art.

Morgen Journal of New York, March 26, '93: Eine Anzahl geistreicher und sachverständiger Aufsätze.

Buffalo (N. Y.) Courier, March 26, '93: Mr. Lombard, during his residence in America, has devoted himself to the spread of sound musical doctrines, and he now stands at the head of one of the largest conservatories in this country. He believed in a principle, and upon the basis of this belief he has worked persistently with the results recorded above. During a period of ten or more years he has written much for print and his articles have always commanded the attention and respect of the musical fraternity. His book contains excellent advice and much information, told in a readable manner. The chapters have such attractive headings that the musician is beguiled into reading their substance even against his intention. For instance his chapter on "Music for the People" is full of suggestive ideas and hints to all. He has very interesting chapters on "Music in Political Economy," and on "National Songs," and those are followed by a chapter which every parent in Buffalo would do well to read. It is entitled, "Train Musicians Early." Mr. Lombard has performed a good service in issuing his book. It will be read by many people who never read a musical publication, because they claim that they are not musical.

Brooklyn (N. Y.) Standard-Union, March 26, '93: A collection of essays in musical matters by Louis Lombard, who is a recognized authority on this subject. Ella Wheeler Wilcox says that in commending this volume she is but doing the cause of music, no less than its distinguished representative, simple justice, and the reader will agree with her.

Buffalo (N. Y.) Express, April 2, '93: Mr. Lombard is an energetic, pushing man, and writes as if neither he nor his readers had much time to spare. Most of his chapters contain emphatic statements of healthy and generally accepted views.

Rochester (N. Y.) Post-Express, April 8, '93: Of decided interest to music lovers.

Buffalo (N. Y.) Review, April 8, '93: Read Lombard's "Observations of a Musician," if you want to spend a profitable and interesting hour. He can say much more in fewer words than any man, big or little, in the profession.

Boston Home Journal, April 8, '93: A writer of fine ability. His essays cover a wide range of subjects connected with music, and display a cultured and practical mind. Students of music especially, will find the book a bright, interesting and helpful companion.

Little Rock (Ark.) Democrat, April 8, '93: Very suitable to the busy man who does not want to wade through fifty pages to get an idea which might be expressed in a few lines.

New York Telegram, April 15, '93: Full of interest and helpfulness; chapters which parents will do well to consider.

Philadelphia Etude, April, '93: A valuable volume by a musical writer of acknowledged ability. It is worthy of a place in every musical library.

New York Musical Courier, March 29, '93: What the Lord did for Mr. Louis Lombard, who weighs only ninety-four pounds, he has done for his dainty little volume. Much has certainly been put in little in both cases. The book is packed with musical truths. A law should be passed compelling "the masses" to read every word of it, in the interest of musical progress. How a foreigner could express so much in such terse yet elegant English is a conundrum to the connoisseur.

Addison F. Andrews, in the *New York Musical Courier*, March 29, '93: Lombard's ability as an original thinker and writer is readily apparent. The fact that he is proficient in six languages causes one to admire all the more his scholarly English.

Auburn (N. Y.) Bulletin, April 15, '93: The gifted author has set forth his ideas in well-written essays. The volume will be read and appreciated by musicians, coming as it does from the pen of a genius.

New York Home Journal, April 19, '93: In "Observations of a Musician," Louis Lombard, the well-known teacher, conductor, composer and critic, discusses music in some of its popular phases, and makes some valuable suggestions for cultivating a taste for it among the people, and as to the best methods of instruction in its science and technique.

Logansport (Ind.) Home Music Journal, April, '93: Interesting observations and facts. The book is from Mr. Lombard's gifted pen, and is worth a careful reading.

Kingston (N. Y.) Daily Tribune, April 27, '93: A neat volume which shows great grace of composition and considerable critical ability.

New York American Bookseller, May 20, '93: Prof. Lombard gives a variety of entertaining and sensible reading, well worth the time and attention of intending pupils and their guardians.

New York Evening Post, May 27, '93: The essays are light without being in the nature of chaff. They are twenty-four plain, short, common-sense five-minute talks on musical topics. The advice given is usually sound and the style entertaining.

New York Tribune, June 8, '93: Louis Lombard gossips on a variety of musical topics in a generally agreeable and sensible manner.

The Critic, New York, May 27, '93: Mr. Lombard displays the usual warmth of the musical temperament in his utterances, and, while his observations are the result of absorbing devotion to his art and earnest thought about it, they are not always couched in judicial language.

Christian Herald, New York, May 31, '93: A compact volume, containing a wide range of expert information.

www.ingramcontent.com/pod-product-compliance
Lightning Source LLC
Chambersburg PA
CBHW021829230426
43669CB00008B/915